Secrets
TO A MAN'S
HEART

michelle
mckinney
hammond

HARVEST HOUSE PUBLISHERS
EUGENE, OREGON

Cover photos © -slav-, Duncan_Andison / iStock

Cover design by Knail

SECRETS TO A MAN'S HEART

Copyright © 2015 Michelle McKinney Hammond
Published by Harvest House Publishers
Eugene, Oregon 97402
www.harvesthousepublishers.com

Library of Congress Cataloging-in-Publication Data
    McKinney Hammond, Michelle.
    Secrets to a man's heart / Michelle McKinney Hammond.
        pages cm
    ISBN 978-0-7369-6487-6 (pbk.)
    ISBN 978-0-7369-6488-3 (eBook)
    1. Men in the Bible. 2. Femininity in the Bible. I. Title.
    BS574.5.M36 2015
    248.8'43—dc23

                                                    2015014553

Printed in the United States of America

        15 16 17 18 19 20 21 22 23 / BP-JH / 10 9 8 7 6 5 4 3 2 1

*To all the women who strive to hear
the hearts of their men,
but sometimes their own heartbeats drown out
their men's voices.*

Acknowledgments

There are so many great men in my life, and I celebrate them all. You know who you are—the list would be far too long for this page. However, there are a few I must note:

- ❧ My two wonderful fathers: George K.A. Hammond and William McKinney
- ❧ My archbishop: Nicholas Duncan Williams
- ❧ My spiritual father link: Pastor Aaron Fruh
- ❧ My big brothers in faith: Pastor Ghandi, Pastor Agu, Pastor Tony Rapu, Pastor Ituah, Pastor Yemi, Pastor Fiifi, Pastor Kofi

These men have impacted my life in ways far too profound to note here. Their lives have spoken far more than their words. They helped me know that great men of integrity really do exist, and there is hope for a woman like me to have lasting love with a man who truly knows and loves God.

I am grateful for you. Thank you.

Contents

What Do Men Really Want?

The question is often asked, "What do men really want?" The answer has remained the same through the years even though situations and circumstances have changed. It's fair to say that there is nothing new under the sun, and that when God created Adam He didn't break the DNA mold. Men still have the same desires. Their hearts beat for the same things: love, honor, and women who have their backs against the odds.

And so it began in the beautiful Garden of Eden. Man and woman walking in divine harmony. Communing with God and with each another. No strife, no misunderstandings, no struggles. They were so in tune with one another they didn't even notice one another's nakedness.

[Enter stage left the serpent.]

After the fall, what was once as natural as breathing became hard labor. The apostle Paul, when comparing the love of a husband for his wife to the love Christ had for His bride (the church), called the union a mystery. Relationships, platonic or romantic, never seem to be free of drama at some point or another. They test the core of our humanity. They reveal what we are truly made of.

And yet these same relationships, when healthy and God-centered, reveal the heart of God toward us. We get an inkling of how He feels when we love and adore Him or ignore and reject Him. The difficulties we face in relationships can always be traced back to how closely we are walking with God. He wired us to reflect His nature, His emotions, and His character. But because our human capabilities fall far short, He uses relationships to shape and mature these qualities in us. Though the fall of mankind disrupted the original plan God had for our relationships, He is in the restoration business. Can utopia be achieved again? No, not until we are one with God in heaven. But I do believe we can experience greater joy in our earthly relationships...if we're willing to do the work to achieve it.

God loves us, and He understands us. (And yes, He loves us even when we do things He doesn't like.) This understanding gives Him the willingness to extend grace toward us. This is why God's Word encourages us to get understanding over all things.[1] Understanding enables us to give grace to the people in our lives and paves the way for deeper communication and harmony. That's what this book is all about: gaining a better understanding of a man's heart.

Men want the same things women want. To be loved. Treasured. Honored. However, they esteem these things using different expressions than we typically do. Yes, men and women are different. Our needs are different. Our strengths are different. Perhaps that is why God created Eve—to balance His creation of Adam. Men and women are different yet equally powerful when we come together according to God's design. Together man and woman become a power couple when they wield their God-given gifts correctly. Relationships are not contests between the sexes, as much of the world has made them out to be. The original design was always about *partnership*, about experiencing the victories of life *together*.

An Intriguing Resource—Men of the Bible

I've often wondered how the men of the Bible felt about their relationships. Consider what transpired between David and Bathsheba, for instance. Or Samson and Delilah. How did these women win their men's hearts? What made King Ahasuerus putty in Esther's hands? Why did Pontius Pilate listen to his wife and wash his hands of condemning Jesus to crucifixion?

If we sat down to talk with these men, what would they tell us about their relationships? About the women in their lives? What would they like to say to women of today regarding love? What secrets and insights about men does God reveal to women through His Word? That is what we're going to explore together as we journey back in time and take a peek into the lives and loves of men of the Bible. We'll discover how men feel...and how they share their hearts, their dreams, their stories, their cares.

Read, learn, and apply, my sister. Heed their stories...and then write your own.

Michelle

The Greatest Gift

Since you aren't dear to me, how shall I address you? At any rate, greetings are of no consequence. Instead I'll simply share my tale. Though I've been called "the father of lies," I will admit to one truth lest this letter to you be misconstrued. I hated them both—Adam and Eve, that is. But this they didn't know. They were also naïve to my history.

You see, I was the exalted one. I was stunningly beautiful, and God considered me to be one of His greatest creations. He admired His handiwork when He looked at me. I was cherished.[1] That is, until I fell from His good graces. I refuse to admit the situation was my own fault or it was my own heart in which a root of iniquity was found.

The flame of rebellion stirred within me. I rose up to ascend to the throne of God. I'd grown weary of collecting praises to deliver to Him. Since I was so splendid, why not keep the praise and worship for myself? I was the one in charge of worship. I led the heavenly choir. [2] I was respected, and honored, and put in charge.

Why do you find it so surprising that I decided I could be like God? That I thought I could establish my own throne? I had a good following among the angels. Many were loyal to me. They would follow me to the ends of the earth, I was sure. And so I led them in war. I never conceived I wouldn't win. A third of the heavenly host rallied to my cause!

But we came face-to-face with Him—with Jesus. Under His watch I was overthrown. I fell like lightning from the heavens.[3] Away from God's grace, from my heavenly estate, from my position as the most-beautiful, most-cherished specimen God had created.

My new form in comparison to those new creations—male and female humans—was insulting. God was so enthralled with the man, Adam, that He actually came down from heaven to speak with him often. He'd never desired that with me. I always had to request an audience with Him. And now He was adding insult to injury by coming down to visit a creation He made a little lower than Himself but higher than me after He pronounced my fate.[4] And they are finite beings! Yessssss, I hated them.

I hated God even more for exalting these creatures over me. For replacing me with subjects created to give Him the worship I wanted, I craved. These human beings were fragile. I would prove how less divine they were by ruining them. I would steal their desire to worship God. I would hurt God by destroying what meant so much to Him. But how? I watched and waited for a way to bring them down—and an opportune time to carry out my plan.

I remember when God first created Adam. Heaven literally held its breath. This creation He crafted with such love. As if throwing pottery on a wheel, He formed this man from the earth. And then God did something I'd never seen Him do. He folded Himself up from beyond the expanse of heaven and, confining Himself within the universe that was once within Him, He submitted Himself to a more limited space so He could enter the earthly realm and be within the reach of this man creature.

This was downright ungodlike behavior! Then He did something that made all of us heavenly beings stand still. He bent down from heaven and seemed to kiss the man. He breathed into Adam, and Adam (and all humans to follow) became a living soul. A living, breathing soul.[5]

God then placed this man into a garden in Eden. The very name "Eden" means "pleasure" or "delight."[6] It was pure utopia for him, I'm sure. You would've called it magical, but it was actually divine. A reflection of heaven in its perfection—yet not quite. All the creatures lived in harmony. The vegetation was lush, and the weather perfect. Mists watered the earth, and peace and beauty prevailed.[7] It was beyond anything that you could ever imagine, and it hasn't existed since. (I'll get to how all of that changed soon.)

In spite of all the beauty God had created around the man, Adam only had eyes for God. I couldn't find an entry to distract him away from his awe-filled worship. And, I admit, God surprised me. He thought it not disdainful to descend to earth in order to converse with Adam. This perplexed all us angels. What was man that God would consider him so? Why the strong attachment? God and Adam walked and talked in the cool of the day in the Garden like they were old friends. God sharing His heart; Adam listening intently.[8]

And then one day it happened. The opportunity I'd been looking for.

After a time, God decided that Adam should no longer be without someone of his own kind. In fact, he couldn't remain alone if he was to fulfill the command God would soon give: be fruitful and multiply. Something...someone...was missing. Every creature in creation had a complementary partner except for Adam. Every creature had a mate for reproduction and to facilitate fruitfulness.

Even most trees and plants had seeds that, when pollinated, would grow and produce fruit. But not Adam. He was alone. Well, not really alone because creation was all around him and God visited often. But Adam didn't have someone to complement him.

And so God created woman. I watched as He gently put Adam to sleep. He opened the side of man, took from his ribs, and fashioned a woman.[9] I must admit she was beautiful. Almost as beautiful as me. I understood why she became Adam's weakness. Once joined to her, why would he want to be separated? I could see it in his eyes, in his demeanor.

Don't get me wrong. Adam still worshipped God, but the man was enthralled with the woman. And she with him. As I watched, I sensed they would worship each other if God was out of the way. The more I pondered this, the clearer my plan became. Obedience to God was the highest form of worship, so any worship diverted from Him would please me.

There was only one way to make that happen—to separate these people from God. I would have to leverage something to get Adam and Eve to do the unmentionable—to disobey God. I decided I would divide and conquer. The woman was new to the game. She seemed a lot more innocent and, thankfully, naïve. She was more moved by feelings and instinct than Adam, which made her more susceptible to being swayed. Adam was more rigid, more bottom line. He knew what God had said, and he would stick to it. But Eve...

I had the feeling I could engage her and get her to see things my way. Once I had Eve eating out of my hand, Adam would be sure to follow. Her influence on him was already evident. It was the perfect plan. I would get to Eve, and then, through her, I'd get to Adam. She was his weakness. And through them I'd get to God.

I waited...watching for the perfect moment. And then it came. It was far easier than I'd imagined. The woman, Eve, welcomed conversing with me. She liked to talk. And sometimes the thing you master turns out to be what causes your downfall. I relied on that in this instance. All it took was one question for the floodgates to open. I asked one question that caused Eve to be suspicious of God. I simply pointed out that He was withholding something from her...something desirable. Did God feel threatened by them? That they might become like Him by partaking of the fruit of the tree in the middle of the Garden?

At first Eve defended God, saying He was just protecting them from hurting themselves or even dying. But her defense of His protection paled in comparison to what I pointed out to her. "Perhaps God is trying to deny you of the same thing He denied me of?" I murmured. I counted on the fact that at the end of the day everyone wants to be their own god. Who wants to serve and be dependent on someone or something who might not put them first or have their best interest at heart?

Never mind that Eve was already like God. If she didn't know that, I certainly wasn't going to tell her. God didn't want them to learn of evil through personal experience, only by knowledge of His word and what He shared with them. The whole withholding angle wasn't exactly a lie. More like a half-truth.

And Eve went for it—hook, line, and sinker. My first fish! By the time I was finished beguiling her, she'd forgotten the generosity of God. All she could see was what He was denying her. So she took and ate the fruit of the tree of knowledge of good and evil.[10] And just as I'd counted on her doing, she gave some to Adam and he also ate. After all, they were one.

Unfortunately my victory was cut short by God Himself. After eating the fruit, immediately Adam and Eve's eyes were opened, and they gazed on their nakedness with horror. They made coverings out of leaves.[11] When they heard the Lord coming, they ran to hide but it was too late. The damage had been done. Their eyes were open. Suddenly they realized they weren't so beautiful. Their perfection was marred and could not be restored. They were ashamed. Disgraced. They'd chosen independence and moved from under the umbrella of God's grace. Yes, they were dis-graced. Yet they were the ones who had willingly dissed the grace of God.

While God waited, giving them a chance to confess, the consequences of their sin set in. Their denial and need to point blame elsewhere disappointed God. I could see that. Trust was broken. Their friendship was shattered. This single act of disobedience that couldn't be undone would lead to another and another. Success!

Until that woman blamed me, and God, of course, knew she was right. The punishment He rendered was more than I could bear. To be sent to a lower state than all those previously beneath me was the final straw.[12] I fell into an abyss of bitterness fueled by my hatred.

My war was no longer just against God. It was now also against mankind—against you and all women and their offspring. I would bruise you in a place of vulnerability. The place in your heart that could affect your walk with God. Reprisal seemed the only course of action I had against the sentence leveled at me. I decided I would take as many humans down with me as I could.

You know what *really* galls me? When *I* sinned, my punishment was eternal. But when Adam and Eve sinned, God sought a solution to redeem them. What kind of love did God have for those creatures? I couldn't comprehend it. I knew I didn't possess it. Envy set in, and I made it my mission to set men and women against each other and against God. To make them sin and fall far short of His glory.

But enough of that. I'd rather dwell on my success. I did such a great job! Every time humans sin, they're choosing *my* way...they're putting me first, in essence. They're helping me pierce the heart of

God with one of my arrows. They willingly become tools in my hands. Not only do they hurt God, but their actions separate them from Him even more. Ha! Their lot becomes the same as mine. Utter darkness that never satisfies their hunger for light.

Many of your troubles aren't really issues with your man. They're because of *my* handiwork. The results of the fall make loving someone difficult. The fight for lordship rages through almost every human relationship on the face of the earth. Such sweet success. As women everywhere desire to take charge and be in charge, the peace God originally designed for couples is shattered. This delights me! Women can never be at true peace with men if they aren't at peace with God.

I must say, I do my work well. I like it when you're oblivious to my influence and ignorant of my devices. The better to deceive you...

Perhaps I've shared too much, but take heed. If you want advice on more than just getting what you want from your man, you shouldn't converse with snakes.

Your partner in crime,

Satan

Man to Woman

A woman who doesn't know her power is destined to misuse it. The world has seized Satan's strategy to distract women from the truth of their significance. The world tells us we're powerless. Not in control. Without honor. Underappreciated. Unrecognized. All attributes that point to "being God" as opposed to partnering with Him in the pursuit of building *His* kingdom rather than our own. God is ultimately in control and deserves all the honor. To try to take away from this puts us in the same mindset that got Satan in trouble.

This train of thinking has fueled the division between men and women. Each party has retreated to their own corners, utilizing their own tools to manipulate one another to get their own way. This has exacerbated the lack of trust that often exists between the sexes. This frame of mind hinders oneness with God, which is the foundation for fruitfulness to occur. By our own determination we decide if we will buy the lies of the enemy of our souls or embrace the truths that God freely gives.

The truth of the matter is that God created us to be powerful. Take a look around you. Every person on the face of the earth arrived through the womb of a woman. Even Jesus did! God created women to assist men in furthering God's kingdom agenda. Without women, men live a one-dimensional life that hinders their ability to be fruit-ful. In God's economy, partnership is essential to get anything done. Individuals and couples partner with God to accomplish what He calls us to achieve. There is power in more than one.

We all have our assignments to keep God's plans moving forward. God designed us as interdependent beings so that no one can accomplish their God-given assignments alone. We need one another for encouragement and help as we use our God-given gifts to accomplish His will.

When a couple is operating as one, as they're called to do by God, they become a wonderful depiction of the kingdom of God. It makes God look good because we see love in action the way God ordained it. This doesn't apply just to married couples either. It applies to our interactions with men on every level—family, busi-ness, church. This healthy interaction makes the people around us hunger and thirst to become part of God's kingdom. This is why Satan works overtime on women. He hates unity. He knows that when a man and a woman are in perfect alignment with each other and with God, moving as one together, they can accomplish anything. If the devil can separate us from God, he can separate us from our men and wreak havoc with our relationships.

The trouble begins when we engage in conversation with the serpent. When we don't keep our emotions and desires submitted to God and keep the lines of communication open with Him, with our significant other, and with the people we have quality relationships with, the door is open for strife and misunderstanding. We are all susceptible; therefore, it is important to know God and His Word regarding you and your situation. Then you can successfully combat the questions of the serpent with declarations of what God has taught you. When Jesus was confronted by Satan in the wilderness, He stood firm in His convictions and proclaimed, "It is written..." A woman submitted to God can, with Jesus' help, resist the devil and make him flee.

The Truth of the Matter

We all make mistakes. We all have struggled in relationships at some point in time. It's easy to listen to the voice of condemnation that proclaims we've messed up and our situation or relationship seems beyond fixing. But God is always simply waiting for us to invite Him into our conversations and decisions on any given matter.

You are not alone. God promises *never* to leave you or forsake you. He will be in the midst of your relationships if you invite Him to be. Remember, a three-strand cord is not easily broken. Your willingness to be transparent with your partner, ask the needed questions, seek the Lord's wisdom, and voice your innermost thoughts will bond you together and make you fruitful. As a team united with

Christ, you can carry out God's commission to "take dominion" and subdue evil in your personal lives and in your community.

When you acknowledge and focus on your power in your man's life and remain submitted to God, you'll experience the joy of harmonious relationships and communion with God. That is the essence of kingdom living.

Matters of the Heart

1. What causes you to question your value as a woman?

2. What examples can you give of a woman making a difference in a man's life?

3. What do you think God wants you to know first and foremost? Why would the serpent not want you to discover this?

The Power of Influence

My dear daughter,

Even though we're generations apart, I consider you my daughter, so I will address you as such. I want to take this opportunity to tell you what I think every father should tell his daughter about becoming a woman. Perhaps if fathers took the time to let their daughters know how powerful they are, the world would be extremely different. I will never be able to explain what took place in the Garden of Eden that afternoon that affected the world forever, but I can tell you what led to later events.

I could feel life coming into my body as God hovered over me and breathed into me.[1] When I opened my eyes, I took in His gaze. His breath within me created a longing for more of Him. And so our friendship began. Father and created being close, intimate friends. Walking and talking in the cool of the day, He spoke to me of His creation. Plans for the future. So many things. When He departed, I waited earnestly for His return. There was a void deep within me when He left that stayed until our next meeting. This time together became what I looked forward to each day.

Was I lonely? Not at all. The Garden around me teemed with life. Creation buzzed daily with excitement, and I marveled at God's handiwork. The wind whispered mysteries about Him. The sun proclaimed His glory. The animals and creatures all gave reverence to Him. There was complete harmony on the earth. No, I wasn't lonely. I was with God and all His creation. My world was full. I felt fulfilled. I wasn't aware of anything being needed except communion with Him.

Then one day God told me to name all of the animals. As I named them one-by-one, I noticed there were two of each kind, and none were like me. I didn't have a partner. My "other" didn't exist. There was no one to share my name. This was a fleeting thought. I was made in God's image, yet I was still coming into the fullness of what that meant. Although I couldn't create the animals, by saying their names, I did determine what they'd be called forever.[2] Almost like when God spoke, the thing was established. It was the first exercise of my authority.

When my mission was completed, sleep overcame me. A deep sleep that felt like a thousand nights had gone by. When I awoke, the most beautiful creature I'd ever seen stood before me. She was like me...but not like me. She wasn't like anything I'd ever seen. And then I felt it. I knew why she was familiar to me. She had come *from* me. She was bone of my bone and flesh of my flesh. I named her woman.[3] We were the same creature but built differently. She seemed to fill me. She filled in the blanks in my thoughts and emotions...yet not exactly. She was a mystery. I was complete *before* she came, but now I had a complement. She was my perfect match. Purposefully fit to me to help me accomplish my God-given assignment: Be fruitful and multiply. Subdue the earth and all that's in it. Have dominion over all living things.[4] She would help me do this. She was my partner.

She finished my sentences, and I hers. It was amazing how

different she was...but so like me at the same time. Her strengths were my weaknesses. My strength her weaknesses. And so it was. I found aspects of myself in her I never knew existed. It was a feeling that intoxicated me. One I did not want to lose. I loved Eve because of how she made me feel and what she added to my world. Suddenly my surroundings were more alive than I'd noticed before. She saw things I didn't see. She added new dimensions to everything. Out of all the things God created, I'm certain she was His masterpiece. The most beautiful. The most irresistible. The most intriguing. Every time I thought I had her figured out, I discovered something else even more wonderful about her. She was an ever-unfolding mystery I couldn't get enough of. God had done His work well.

Eve and I were always near each other. Until that fateful day. Until the serpent engaged my beautiful wife in conversation. By the time I reached her, she'd already tasted the fruit God had forbidden us to eat. I was horrified. I knew what God had said about this particular tree. But now I wondered why it would be so bad. There my woman stood with a look of great pleasure on her face as she extended the fruit to me. Her smile said it all. This fruit is good to eat. That was all I needed! For a brief moment I forgot God's instructions. I wanted to be part of whatever Eve did, and this would be no exception. I took the fruit and ate.[5] But I didn't feel the pleasure I saw on her face. The moment I ingested it, I felt a deep sense of dread.

Suddenly Eve and I realized we were naked. We quickly got large fig leaves to cover ourselves. My anguish grew stronger when I sensed God approaching. It was the time of day when He usually visited. Eve obviously felt it too. The look of fear on her face reflected my thoughts. We ran and hid from God, knowing we would have to go to Him when He called again. After all, where could we go that His presence wouldn't be?

Sure enough, He called. I came out of hiding and explained I was ashamed of my nakedness. He asked me immediately, "Who told you that you were naked?" *Who indeed?* I thought. No one had told us. Not even the serpent. I shivered under this line of questioning. I searched for an answer that made sense. There wasn't one. My nakedness hadn't bothered me before I ate of the fruit. Nothing had changed *around* me, so the change must have been *within* me. I had changed. My heart condition had changed. God remained the same, but I didn't. And the painful difference was glaring. Damage had taken place.

God stood close to Eve and me, yet I felt a yawning distance between us. I didn't know how to cross that great divide. Suddenly He felt so far away, and I felt so lonely. The distance had also grown between Eve and me. This was when I realized it was our mutual connection to God that had given us the ability to be in complete harmony. All of a sudden I was a bit wary of her. Was she the catalyst of all this trouble? But perhaps it was really God's fault. After all, He was the one who gave her to me.

I wasn't clear on exactly whom I could logically blame. Eve had broken our trust. She who was created to assist me in carrying out all that God commanded had drawn me into disobedience.

God held me responsible for our disobedience. He'd placed the woman within my protection, and I'd failed her as I had failed God. When He said, "Because you listened to your wife," all I could do was hang my head in shame. I should have stopped her. I was supposed to cover and protect her. I should never have left her open to the serpent's suggestion. If I had been present to hear the conversation, perhaps I could have refuted the serpent's words.

Eve erred, but I didn't have to follow suit and eat of the fruit. Yet the thought of acting separately from her was more unbearable than the thought of going against what God had said. Perhaps it was because I didn't realize the full ramifications of my actions. Though God had said we would die if we ate of the fruit, death was preferable to being separated from Eve. There. I've said it. She was that much a part of me, so I failed to count the cost.

God did not let the cost escape me...or Eve. We would pay dearly for our mistake. The ground would no longer yield readily to my authority. God said I would have to work by the sweat of my brow to sow and reap what once came easily. It would be a hard life, and one that was foreign to me. We'd never had to depend on my labor before. And God said Eve would experience labor pains when she birthed children. The children we wanted so much would give her great physical pain. Animosity would be between the serpent and Eve. From now on it would be war between the serpent and our offspring. There would be damaging blows to all concerned.

The price seemed too much to bear. And yet in the midst of our disobedience, God did a gracious thing that made us more in awe of His love. He made a sacrifice and covered us in skins before He led us out of the Garden. He covered us—our sin and our shame.

The depth of what we'd done finally sank in as we saw the entrance to the Garden close behind us. The future seemed bleak. Heaven on earth no longer existed.

So, my daughter, Eve and I owe you and the rest of mankind an apology. You'll never realize the full extent of our regret. I can only say that God is most wise. Heed and believe Him. Following His will is the only way to possess peace, joy, and deep fulfillment. And nothing in this life is worth forfeiting that.

Thankful for His grace,

Adam

Man to Woman

This is what many women seem not to know. Their men crave their nearness. Their connection means a lot. A man literally lives to be joined to his wife (once he has located her). Their oneness strengthens him. His ability to trust her means even more. He needs to know his woman has his back. And though she needs him, she is strong enough to stand on her own in times of his absence. Part of being one with him is representing him in the right light. Knowing his mind and making decisions that would benefit you both when he's gone. Making wise decisions is something singles need to learn how to do *before* getting married. This is why communication is key.

Who knows what really happened that afternoon in the Garden? There are many different theories. One group says Adam wasn't present when Eve had her discussion with the serpent. Adam's absence left her open to the snake's deceptive conversation. Another view is that Adam was indeed present and didn't interject what he knew so he didn't stop Eve from eating, and then he willfully followed her into sin. Either way it went, Adam was held responsible for Eve's sin though she also was held liable.[6] The consequences to them both damaged the state of relationships between men and women clear up to present day.

I believe that part of the curse that day was that Eve would always desire more from her husband than he could give, and that her desire would get the best of her. She (and every mother since) would also suffer the pain of childbearing and the fear of watching her children struggle against the offspring of the serpent. Every mother wants the best for her children, and watching them struggle with temptation and other worldly assaults can be hard on a mother's heart. The pain of delivering a child is only the beginning.

For Adam, having to now sweat to produce fruit was a direct challenge to his manhood. And the struggle to be fruitful in the areas that affirm his identity is a dilemma every modern man faces. His identity is wrapped up in what he is able to produce and how well he can provide for his woman. Even as singles, men are judged by how productive and fruitful they are professionally. A man's desire to protect his woman and meet her expectations is extremely strong. In his relationship with his woman, a man fears feeling as if he can never qualify or be enough. It's his greatest relationship worry next to whether he can trust her.

Man is far more vulnerable to woman than we think.

The Truth of the Matter

No woman can be all things. In order to become a Proverbs 31 woman—the kind of woman who inspires blessings from her husband and children—the fear of the Lord must be present in her life. It must be the ruling force that encourages her to gain and possess the wisdom she needs to navigate through life in such a way that her husband trusts her completely. This type of woman inspires him to be fruitful and helps equip him to be the man God designed him to be.

A woman who fears the Lord doesn't entertain serpents in any form. Whether this involves spiritual attacks against the mind, or assaults on the flesh in the form of temptation, or the counsel of the ungodly or those not grounded in God, or in the lack of good intentions, the woman who fears God is able to stand firm in discernment and make wise choices for her loved ones and herself.

God gave woman the unique gift of influence. This gift was to empower her to empower the man in her life to accomplish his God-given purpose. This literally makes the man and woman a divine "power couple." Together they bear rich fruit that affects their world at large. "The two shall become one." Single women need to know the power of their influence on the men in their world as well. Speaking into the lives of your friends, brothers, and coworkers by giving them valuable input that inspires them to fruitfulness spiritually as well as naturally is part of what we do as women, whether married or not.

Knowing where your true strength lies and not struggling to be god is the key to success. God already created you to be like Him. What you can't do, He will do for you. As you submit yourself to Him, He'll give you the grace to be all you should be. In Him you live, and move, and have being. All things will be accomplished through His Spirit at work in you. In that you can rest assured...and so can the man in your life.

Matters of the Heart

1. In what ways does the man in your life disappoint you? Which of these expectations are misplaced?

2. In what ways do you affect your man and his ability to accomplish things?

3. What can you do to be a more positive influence in your man's life?

The Beauty of Submission

My dear daughter,

What I will share with you is an adventure that would not have been possible if not for my wife. When God called me to step out in faith to journey to another land, I didn't know how I would broach the topic with my wife, Sarai. Haran had been our home for quite a while, and now God was asking me to venture out beyond my comfort zone. How would I explain to Sarai that I felt compelled to obey even though I didn't know where we were going? I was asking her to trust my capacity to hear from God. What if I was wrong? What if I misunderstood God? We would be bidding farewell to all that was known to us and held dear. All that felt safe. Most of our family and friends. And yet I knew for certain that a longing for something more had been deposited in my spirit.

God promised that He would make of me a mighty nation.[1] What a compelling promise! He also asked for my obedience, so I chose to move out by faith. Sarai was in agreement, and we started out on the experience of a lifetime. My nephew Lot and his wife joined us, along with all our household workers.

Sarai was amazing during this time. Looking back on some of the foolish things I did, I marvel at her steadfast support. Not once but twice she yielded to my advice that she pretend to be my sister so I might avoid trouble.[2] I wasn't really asking her to lie. She was my half sister. But the greater truth was that she was my wife. I feared that because of her beauty, the men of the lands we traveled through would dispose of me to secure her for themselves. And it wasn't just my own skin I thought of. I couldn't bear the thought of what she might be subjected to if I was done away with. My Sarai faithfully complied with my requests.

I thank God for His tender mercies. He shielded and protected Sarai while she was kept behind other men's walls. When it was discovered she was indeed my wife, the rulers sent us away—but not before loading us with various gifts, which increased my wealth substantially. And with Sarai I was already the richest man in the world. She was so beautiful. She could have her pick of any man, and she chose to follow me!

Her love for me was evident. It made me want to be a better man for her. I felt helpless when I couldn't give her the one thing she so badly wanted. Had I not heard God correctly? Had He not promised to make me the father of many nations? Year after year we wondered at this promise...and waited. Every now and then God would reassure me that He was going to do it. *When* was the question.

I was surprised at Sarai's suggestion that I take her maid Hagar to try to produce an heir. What a sacrifice Sarai was making! I knew how much it would mean to her to be the mother of my children. That she would give up such an important position to fulfill my desire for an heir and her desire to be a mother was humbling. Her love for me was beyond my understanding. Perhaps I should have said no to her idea. Had I known the consequences for the rest of the world—the suffering that would come—because of my decision, I surely would have done differently. The conflicts between Sarai and Hagar, and then between my sons, Ishmael and Isaac, were great and seemingly unending. This made me exceedingly sad.

When Hagar announced that she was with child, I could tell by the look on Sarai's face that her lack of ability to have a child cut deeply into her heart. I would have given everything I owned in exchange for the pain I saw in her eyes. Yet she accepted that perhaps this was God's way of doing what He'd foretold. That continued until Hagar began to despise Sarai and fancy herself as the woman of the house. She became rude and disrespectful, adding insult to my Sarai's injury. This Sarai couldn't bear. After all, she'd literally stepped aside for my benefit. Her young slave now overstepped her boundaries. It was the first time I saw Sarai become so irritated. Pain has a way of translating to anger. (Perhaps because anger makes us feel strong in the midst of our pain, though it only masks it temporarily.)

Hagar ran away. Sarai had a small reprieve and peace was restored, but the Lord sent Hagar back. For this I was thankful! Even though having a child with Hagar wasn't my idea, Ishmael was my son. I fretted over his welfare. I loved him because he was my flesh and blood. I settled in my heart that he would be my heir.

Shortly after Hagar and Ishmael returned, God again promised me that I would be a father of many nations.[3] That He'd do what He'd first said. He changed Sarai's name to Sarah, and reiterated that *she* would bear my true heir.[4] God said Sarah would be the mother of nations, and kings would be in her lineage.[5] He also promised that Ishmael, my son with Hagar, would also be a mighty nation. What more could I ask for! (I did wonder how this could be true considering my advanced age.) I trusted God with all my heart and dared to believe His word to me. Every male in my household was circumcised according to God's instruction as a sign of the covenant He made with me.[6]

A year passed and I was visited by messengers from God who confirmed that a child borne by Sarah would indeed be coming.[7] Sarah laughed at this thought, but I'm sure it was a mixture of hope and fatigue.[8] My wife had grown weary of anticipating what seemed to be impossible at our advanced ages. But finally the day came when God opened her womb and Isaac, the child of God's promise, arrived! Sarah's joy couldn't be contained.[9]

All was finally well—or so I thought.

Sarah didn't like Ishmael teasing Isaac, so she said that Hagar should take her son and leave. I struggled with this decision until God spoke and told me to release them. So I loaded them with provisions and sent them on their way.[10] It was like a knife in my heart. But Sarah had always sacrificed for me, and now I would sacrifice for her. I would never purposely do anything that would rob her of her joy.

As the years passed, I prayed Isaac would find a wife as good as his mother. She had been my rock, my supporter, and my cheerleader. And not just a good wife, but a friend. When Sarah died, I mourned even as her memory filled me with joy. Without her, I dare say I would not have become the man I am nor acquired what I did. Perhaps it was Sarah's faith in God that freed her to follow me as I trusted Him. The fact that she trusted God and trusted me to hear from God made me draw closer to Him lest I fall prey to my own flesh and lead her astray. Yes, at a point her faith wavered, but He who promised was faithful to deliver all He'd spoken. We both pressed past our humanity to act on faith for that promise from God, and it came to pass.

Why do I share this story with you? To let you know how important it is to not only trust God but to trust God to work in and through your mate and the other significant people He's placed in your life for you to walk with. You can build a person's faith or destroy it by your response to what is shared with you. Take this from me as a loving father giving you a great secret: Dare to have faith in God. He will never lead you awry.

Still believing in God,

Abraham

Man to Woman

When it comes to romantic relationships, a man longs to be his woman's hero. To lead her through uncharted territory and pave the way for her dreams to come true. He wants to provide for her and protect her. This is confirmation of who he is as a man.

Your man needs your trust and willingness to be his partner through all the twists and turns of life. The trust in your eyes encourages him. Your quiet assurances spur him on to achieve greatness. What you say contributes to what can make or break him. If you're single, you can develop this influence through your male friends, brothers, and coworkers.

Your quiet encouragement or harsh criticism and doubt-filled questions can inspire and compel someone or paralyze and destroy him. What if Sarah had said no when Abraham announced they were moving? What if she refused to cooperate with him as they traveled? What if she hadn't been willing to try one more time for the child God promised? God's plans come to fruition as we partner with Him in faith and obedience.

The woman in a man's life must know that she is a "destiny" partner. That her relationship isn't a personal achievement but an assignment meant to bring glory to God and further the agenda of His kingdom. As a wife honors her spouse, her husband is further empowered to be the man God created him to be. The marvelous gift a woman has to nurture faith, courage, and strength in her man is undeniable when she applies her loving touch to his world. A woman must let a man be a man. She needs to release and encourage him to follow the principles and the call of God. This leads him to cleave to her and to partner with her in achieving both their dreams.

Together with God, they can birth something that has an impact that reaches beyond their personal spheres and into the world at large. As a wife submits to God first and then to her husband as he receives direction from the Lord, they become fruitful together. Submission is a powerful tool that solidifies a couple as a team God can greatly use as they move forward in agreement, deferring to one another as needed.

Whether single or married, we should always remember that submission puts us in position to be blessed at work, in society, and in our homes. Dismissal or denigration of authority creates chaos and disorder. But as we submit one to the other according to our positions and strengths, we become fruitful and victorious on every level.

God created us to be fruitful in this adventure we call life. Every "partnering" on His part is strategic in building His kingdom and a people who will serve Him and glorify Him. This is accomplished through individuals and couples as they say yes to Him. As a single woman, sister, and friend, you can be instrumental in building up others to complete their God-given assignments to be powerful contributors to God's plan. As a wife, you're instructed to submit to your husband. Though some of our greatest goals and desires might delay in coming, we must all encourage and build each other up. The greatest miracles are birthed from the greatest and longest trials.

Keep in mind that your spouse is a vessel God uses to get you to see Him as the ultimate Provider and Protector. Your primary focus needs to be taken off the man and, instead, be placed on God, the Author and Finisher of every adventure.

Matters of the Heart

1. What is your attitude toward submission? In what ways can it be powerful?

2. What are your greatest fears in yielding to the leadership of another?

3. In what ways do you feel God wants to use you in partnership with your spouse or a brother in the Lord?

The Heart of a Servant

My dear,

What I share with you is vital. Looking down through time, I stand amazed at all that has transpired to deceive women about the power of service. While many people long for partners and love, I see generations of women unwilling to give of themselves or serve others. Why is this important? I was the one my boss, Abraham, called to seek a bride for his son Isaac. I felt privileged to serve Abraham in this special way.

I was the eldest servant in his household. I served him all my life, and I remained faithful to him and his family.[1] I was there when both Ishmael and Isaac were born. I witnessed firsthand the struggles between Sarah and Hagar. My heart went out to Hagar when she was sent away, but I also knew much of it was of her own doing. She'd forgotten her place as a servant and lost sight of the value of serving. After being singled out by Sarah for Abraham, Hagar felt work was beneath her. In the end she lost her standing altogether.

The trouble started after Sarah encouraged her husband, Abraham, to sleep with Hagar in hopes that she would bear an heir for them. Hagar was, perhaps, the world's first surrogate mother. Sarah had tried for years to bear a child. Although Abraham told her God had promised to give them countless descendants, Sarah's faith floundered as the years went by. Perhaps it wasn't through her body the child would come, she reasoned. She willingly released her desire to bear a child herself for the sake of Abraham by telling him to have a child with Hagar.

But Hagar grew proud after she conceived. She saw herself as equal in stature to Sarah. There seemed to be no end to her haughtiness and lack of respect. She lorded her pregnancy over Sarah again and again. Hagar was going to be the mother of Abraham's heir, not Sarah.

Sarah lashed out to put Hagar back in her place, but there was no going back for Hagar. Surely Abraham would protect her, she thought. She couldn't bear to be regarded as only a servant. She felt it a great injustice to not be accorded a privileged position. As Hagar's pride grew, so did Sarah's abuse.

Hagar eventually ran away but soon came back. She told me in hushed tones that God told her to return and that she was promised she'd bear a son who would be great in his own right—the father of countless others.[2] God saw her affliction and told her she must submit to Sarah. This Hagar did, but I could tell her heart wasn't in it.

Hagar gave birth to a son, and Abraham named him Ishmael as God had ordained.[3] Abraham was so happy that even Sarah became quiet, although she remained watchful.

Ten or so years went by, and then three extraordinary visitors came. They said Sarah would bear a child. Sarah laughed. For her this notion was past being spoken of anymore. Abraham had his heir in Ishmael, and she'd made peace with herself that this was how life would be. She laughed, and the visitors questioned her lack of faith.

And then it happened! Miracle of miracles—Sarah conceived! This time her laughter was not borne out of incredulity. No, it came from a place of joy that couldn't be contained.

I noticed that Hagar was feeling diminished as she struggled with where she fit in. I believe her bitterness took root in Ishmael's heart too. In the end, their discord cost them dearly. For now there was even more tension between Sarah and Hagar. The two women were very protective of their sons.

When Isaac was born, all the attention shifted to him. To this child of promise. To this miracle. To this obvious display of God's favor. The anger in Hagar's heart resurfaced and was passed on to her son.

When Sarah noticed that Ishmael was teasing Isaac, she grew concerned. She went to Abraham and said, "Get rid of that slave woman and her son, for that woman's son will never share in the inheritance with my son Isaac."[4] It broke Abraham's heart to see them go. After all, Ishmael was his son, was part of his flesh. But God assured Abraham that Ishmael would also be a nation.[5] This gave the patriarch peace. He knew this was the way things were to be. God had told him that his child of promise would come from Sarah and him, not from Hagar and him.

Perhaps if Hagar had better understood the power of possessing a serving heart, she could have remained in Abraham's household. Ishmael and Isaac might have grown up as caring brothers. Who knows what the world would look like today if that had happened. But it wasn't to be.

I never understood Hagar. Her disdain of her position. I counted it an honor to serve Abraham. I knew that in my own way I empowered him to accomplish what he did. He could paint bigger pictures because I took care of the minute details. This was my contribution to his life, and it wasn't a small one. More importantly, as I served him, I gained his trust. So much so that in his old age and after Sarah had passed away, Abraham chose me to seek a wife for Isaac. This was a great honor. He entrusted the selection of his daughter-in-law to me. Only someone held in high regard would be given such a significant assignment. Even though I was a servant by position, I was trusted and respected for my service. This was the advantage I tried to get Hagar to see, but she didn't get it.

A Bride for Isaac

I set off to the land of Aram Naharaim, where Abraham's extended family resided, to search for a bride for Isaac. Uppermost in my mind was that she should have the heart of a servant. When I reached Nahor, I prayed and asked God to give me a clear sign regarding the woman I was to choose.[6] I said that when I asked a young woman for a drink of water, the one chosen for Isaac would offer to water my camels as well. Then I would know she was the right one. This test would also make it clear if the woman was strong, industrious, charitable, and not given to pride.

Before I finished praying a beautiful young lady showed up at the well where I was. I asked her to set down her water jar and give me a drink. She did so and offered to water my camels. I watched her go about this task enthusiastically. I asked her who her family was, and I discovered she was of the family of Abraham! I was overwhelmed by the faithfulness of God. I bowed down and gave Him praise.[7]

Rebekah invited me to her home, saying they had room for me and my companions, along with plenty of fodder for our camels. Upon arriving, there was quite a jubilation as I shared with them the welfare of Abraham and his household. Rebekah was happily serving and being quite the hostess, which confirmed to me that she was the right wife for Isaac. I knew she'd be just what the young man needed after the death of his mother. This young woman would be a comfort to him and serve him well.

I explained my mission, and Rebekah's family members gave their blessing. Rebekah agreed to go with me...to leave her family behind to embrace a man she didn't know. I marveled at her willingness to serve and her bold faith. Yes, God answered my prayer! I knew Isaac would approve of this woman!

When we were almost home, we passed a field where Isaac was working. He came to greet us, and the moment he saw Rebekah the light in his eyes said it all. When we got to his home, Isaac took her into his tent and loved her.

I had completed my mission and was well pleased that I'd been honored with such a special task.

My dear friend, whether you're praying to find the man of your dreams, you've already found your mate, you're working at a job that proves challenging, or you're simply longing for a great friend in your life, never overlook the benefits of serving others. A heart willing to serve attracts goodness.[8]

Seek to serve, and life will serve you well.

Your humble servant,

Eliezer

Man to Woman

A woman who has a heart to serve always gets a man's attention. Though a man appears to be strong and in control, he is still quite vulnerable. It takes a lot for him to trust a woman and release himself into her care. He depends on her for encouragement, well-being, and support.

Today, "taking care of a man" is a lost art. Independence has been rooted firmly in the psyches of a great number of women. And yet many women don't raise their sons to live independently. This creates a huge disconnect between what women are willing to do and what men expect. Most men appreciate women who have a domestic touch, but women are leaving homemaking by droves as they pursue careers far from the home. There is truth in adages such as "The way to a man's heart is through his stomach."

Friend, let's not allow our dreams of professional achievement to rearrange who we are as women. After all, our arms can't hold accomplishments. Some women believe they don't *need* men. Economic liberation has perpetuated this line of thinking, but God created us to need companionship and love.

And consider this: The person God has chosen for your mate needs your care and support in special ways only you can provide. These special touches are things only a wife can provide in a manner that will be deeply felt by her husband. The more a wife seeks to serve her husband, the more her husband seeks to cover his wife. Her care of him creates a deepened sense of responsibility for him to take good care of her—and not just financially, but also emotionally, physically, and spiritually.

Yes, times have changed, but men's hopes remain the same. I believe the desire for women who will nurture and care for them in selfless ways has been placed within their hearts by God Himself. Therefore, it is not an unrealistic desire. At the end of the day, this is what everyone desires. A woman in love wants to nurture her mate. And as she serves him, she'll be rewarded and called blessed.

The Truth of the Matter

Although Sarah had servants, she called Abraham "lord," a term of respect and honor. This speaks volumes about their relationship. She was his wife, and she sought to serve him. He also loved her deeply, and not just because of her physical beauty, which was acclaimed. Sarah's heart and attitude also garnered Abraham's respect and care. Small wonder Eliezer would insist on seeking the heart of a servant in the woman selected for Isaac. Isaac had seen this servant-heart perspective in his mother, and her example would set the standard for his expectations of a wife.

Because many mothers raise their sons without teaching them homemaking skills, boys grow up expecting the same treatment they saw their mothers give to their husbands and to them. I believe we all agree that if someone serves us with love and devotion, that person, in turn, earns our hearts and trust.

When people seek to make us feel significant by positioning themselves to serve us, it speaks volumes about how they esteem us. Jesus thought it not robbery to come to earth as a mortal man to seek, save, and serve lost humanity even though He was considered royalty in heaven. He washed His disciples' feet as a servant would. Peter was horrified and tried to stop Him, but Jesus told him, "Unless I wash you, you have no part with me."[9] Peter than asked that he be washed completely by Jesus.

Jesus is the ultimate example of the power of servanthood. He is a servant leader. He understands that an excellent leader needs the heart and willingness to serve. People who serve by choice are powerful, effective, and influential. They literally hold the lives of the ones they serve in their hands. Don't let ego and pride deceive you into believing there is no honor in serving. We ascend as high as we're willing to bend. Jesus is our Lord and Savior because of His willingness to bend low enough to retrieve us from our lowly estate. We love Him because of what He has done, what He is doing, and what He will do for us.

In all our relationships, whether at home or in the marketplace, we need to appreciate and participate in the power of serving others so we can experience its rewards. Offering to put in the extra effort of watering a man's camels eventually led to Rebekah meeting the man of her dreams and embracing an amazing life.

Why not consider what nurturing a heart of service will gain for you? Remember: God sees and blesses.

Matters of the Heart

1. What is your attitude toward serving the man in your life? And what about serving others?

2. How do you respond when your acts of service aren't reciprocated?

3. Who do you look to for rewards from your service?

The Way of a Woman

My dear daughter,

When my mother passed away, I was beside myself. She'd been the main woman in my life. She adored me and championed me. She spoke into my life. And now she was gone. Then my father, Abraham, decided it was time for me to marry. I couldn't imagine the void my mother left in my heart being filled by anyone, but from the moment I met Rebekah I loved her!

I'll never forget the first time I saw her. It was evening, and I went out to a field to meditate.[1] I think I felt her presence before I saw her. I turned to see a caravan of camels coming across the horizon. A woman on a camel got down and came to me. What a vision of beauty she was! She smiled and my life changed. Comfort and joy washed over me. It was as if I'd known her forever.

Later, when my father's servant Eliezer relayed how he'd found her, how gracious she'd been, and what a heart of service she had, I could see why he was taken with her. Truly God was continuing His faithfulness toward me by taking away the sting of my mother's death and filling my life with love. I was forty, and that number of years didn't bypass me. Indeed it was the end of a season of trial. With Rebekah, a new life awaited.

I suppose life is full of challenges, and no one escapes them. Twenty years went by before Rebekah bore our children. I prayed for her as I saw the disappointment in her eyes each time her hopes were dashed by the monthly visitation of her menses. God heard my prayer and answered above and beyond our expectations! Rebekah became pregnant. She was having a rough time, so she asked God about it. He revealed she had two nations in her womb; two peoples who would be divided, one would be stronger than the other, and the elder would serve the younger.

Rebekah indeed gave birth to twins. The first one came out with red hair all over his body. We called him Esau. The second was holding onto the first one's heel for dear life, so we called him Jacob. Esau became a skilled hunter, while Jacob preferred to take care of business and stay close to home. Jacob was clearly a mama's boy. Oh, how Rebekah loved Jacob. But I loved Esau. He was a mighty hunter and cooked fine meals for us. [2]

Perhaps because Esau was a man who hunted flesh, he became one who was led by his physical body. I was saddened when I learned Esau sold his birthright to Jacob for a serving of stew because Esau was hungry and tired. Perhaps I should have paid more attention to that problem, but it got lost in the turmoil as I focused on how to take care of my family in the midst of a terrible famine.

God, in His infinite kindness, appeared to me and gave me instructions on where to move. He also established the same covenant with me that He had with my father, Abraham. God said He would establish me in the land, and my offspring would be as numerous as the stars of heaven. My descendants would be a blessed people.

We settled in Gerar, but I feared the men of the country would kill me to take Rebekah because she was so beautiful, so I told her to say she was my sister. But Abimelech, the king of the Philistines, saw us laughing and flirting and confronted me regarding the true nature of our relationship. The king told his people to let us live in peace, and so we stayed in the land and prospered. I was grateful to Rebekah for not making this a difficult time. She walked with me and championed me. We grew in wealth, and God blessed me a hundredfold. Soon we were the envy of those around us. My family lacked for nothing.

Or so I thought...until Esau allowed his flesh to rule him again. He married two foreign women, who became the bane of Rebekah's and my existence. I was disappointed, but Esau was still my son. I loved him. And I know Rebekah loved him too, but perhaps it was the words the Lord had given her before the twins were born that made her have a predisposition to lean more toward Jacob. Whatever the reason, I should have dealt with it. Esau's foreign wives didn't help. In fact, they made Rebekah more determined to see the prophecy spoken over Jacob come true. As nurturing as she was to me, she was fiercely protective of Jacob's future.

I was saddened that Rebekah sought to fulfill what God had spoken to her. Her deceit cost us dearly. I don't know why she didn't come to me about Jacob and Esau and the prophecy. I sometimes wonder what the outcome would've been if we'd discussed more what the Lord had said concerning Jacob and Esau. Perhaps I wouldn't have listened and insisted on giving Esau the blessing anyway. Nevertheless, Rebekah decided to make sure Jacob got the blessing. She showed him how to deceive me so he would get the patriarchal blessing. Jacob disguised himself as Esau. My eyes were dim so I couldn't see. Though I thought the voice was different, I couldn't really tell. He smelled and felt like Esau. And so I blessed him. I didn't realize until Esau came that I'd given the blessing to the wrong son.

Poor Esau was heartbroken. But he had despised his birthright by bartering it for stew. He had married foreign women. He seemed not to hold sacred what I did, but now he wanted my blessing.

Since Jacob had gotten the blessing by deception was it really a blessing? Rebekah had broken my trust and set our son up for unnecessary hardship by teaching him to deceive. She then suggested we send Jacob away to get a bride so he wouldn't marry the same type of women his brother had. But it was really because she knew Esau's heart was hardened against Jacob. I later learned Esau planned to kill his brother because of what had transpired. It broke my heart. Deception always causes division. And so we sent Jacob away. I knew I might never see him again.

If Rebekah and I had communicated better, I'm sure the prophecy would have come to pass without human intervention. I'm saying this to you because it is a woman's way to desire to be all things to her man. To do everything and try to make sure that the right things happen in the lives of her loved ones. Be careful not to step into God's shoes. Manipulation will not win or keep your man's love. Your capacity to help him feel loved and heard will.

A loving reminder,

Isaac

Man to Woman

A man looks to a woman for comfort and for security. He needs to know he can trust his woman with the things that are important to him. To know she will be in his corner supporting his decisions or helping him gain clarity when he gets off track. While the man is the head of the home, the woman sets the atmosphere. She can even change the direction the man is going in based on how she positions herself. She is the neck connecting the body to the head so the husband and wife move as one. She can either promote a healthy connection or a dysfunctional disconnection. Her influence will have a profound effect on the legacy they create as a couple or as a family.

A man wants to know his woman has his back after he's made a decision. Trust is broken if he discovers he was deceived or manipulated by his partner. This breach is hard to repair. The couple may stay together, but the disappointment of betrayal hangs like a veil between them. It can kill the love that once existed.

Two people can find themselves merely existing instead of creating a vibrant life together. When this occurs, repentance and the Spirit of God are needed to reconstruct the bond between them. The key to any lasting relationship with your man is creating a safe place for his heart, his dreams, and even his fears. Your ability to comfort him in the midst of his storms gains his trust and reliance.

Your devotion encourages him to return your love and care. Your selfless nature draws him to you. Your partnership with him in handling your relationship and life are essential to his well-being.

In a marriage situation, his expectation is that his wife enforces the laws he establishes in his home, so that their children learn to respect his authority and honor their mother. He expects his wife to set the home atmosphere as one that promotes unity, respect, honor, and consideration among the entire family. There is no place for competition or sibling rivalry in a home when a woman understands the needs of her man. She knows that peace is essential to his well-being. The husband and children who rise to call the woman of the house blessed are those who have blossomed under her care and have good fruit to show for it.

The Truth of the Matter

How could a romance such as the one between Rebekah and Isaac come to such conflict? I'll tell you how. Anytime we women decide to take matters into our own hands to fulfill what God has spoken, the end of the story is always a disaster. Sometimes when a woman feels her partner isn't strong enough to make decisions, she's tempted to rise up and "make it happen." This is death to her relationship with her man. A promise from God doesn't mean He wants you to take on the responsibility of causing it to come to pass. Humanity corrupts divinity. When Rachel felt the need to help her son deceive his father, she was showing the depth of her lack of faith in God's ability to do what He said He would do.

Favoritism shown toward a specific child in a family encourages those who aren't favored to war and compete against the other. Envy creates strife and every evil work.[3] This is not the picture of the family God had in mind. He wants families on earth to reflect the unity of heaven through the support of one another. When children are involved, the mother sets the tone of how they interact with one another. Whether they become unified or rivals will depend largely on how she nurtures her charges.

I find it obvious that since Esau didn't feel the love of his mother, he sought out and married women who weren't like her. Had his love for his mother been strong, he would have searched for a woman who was like his mother. We reap what we sow. When Rachel aided Jacob in deceiving his father, she encouraged an attitude of deception that followed Jacob throughout his life. One thing simply led to another. In her effort to keep her relationship with Jacob strong, she lost it. Though God's Word doesn't tell us if Rachel ever regretted her decision, I figure she had to because she never saw Jacob again. She helped create a divide that made Jacob a fugitive from his brother.

Though the story ends well for Jacob, I wonder how much of

what he went through was really necessary. Couldn't God have orchestrated another way to bring him into the same position in life, a way free from deception, painful alliances, and separation? Generally speaking, trials in life are inevitable, but some are optional. Some of the beds we feel forced to lie in are of our own making.

We must be honest about our motives when interacting with our significant others and our families. Selfish agendas are never good foundations for relationships, especially ones we want to last and weather the test of time. Transparency and accountability must prevail for love to be sustained and honor to remain within a relationship. We need to walk in the knowledge that God is well able to keep His word without our help. We need to trust that whatever He speaks into our lives will never break the trust of those we love.

Matters of the Heart

1. What is the hardest thing about waiting on the promises of God?

2. How do you respond when your partner or those around you don't seem to have the capacity to understand what has been placed on your heart?

3. How can you help your man feel like you partner *with* him in areas that require great faith?

What Beauty Can't Do

My dear,

I pray what I share with you will help you in the area of your esteem. I know you feel pressured to be beautiful and desirable in order to win the heart of a man, but let me tell you that it takes so much more.

Yes, it's true when I first met Rachel I was moved by her beauty. It was...how do you say it? Love at first sight. She was so beautiful, so vibrant and alive. She took my breath away. She was like a vision. Some shepherds pointed her out to me, and I watched as she came to the well driving her father's sheep before her. While the shepherds waited for the other herders to congregate in order to roll away the stone at the mouth of the well, I singlehandedly removed it and watered all of Rachel's sheep.[1] Where I found the strength, I don't know. Love makes a man do crazy things. Since she was my kin, I boldly kissed her in public—so happy was I to see her and hear of my family. But it was more than that. My heart leaped within me. I had found my soul mate in that moment.

I was warmly embraced by her father and brothers and, yes, even her sister, Leah. I was so pleased I'd found a home and the woman I loved all in the same day. Every time I looked at Rachel I felt like singing. I couldn't explain it. Nothing was the same. Work didn't feel like work. Just to be near her made everything so much more pleasant. After I had been working for her father and my uncle for a month, Laban asked me what I would take for wages. I asked for Rachel. I agreed to work seven years to earn her hand. And I have to tell you, it felt like a day. The anticipation of spending the rest of my life with her became my all-consuming passion. I counted the days even though they were as minutes. I loved her so much.

And then the day finally came when I would claim her as my bride. I was elated. Intoxicated. So happy I thought I would burst. Rachel would be mine...all mine. But after the nuptials, I awakened to find her sister Leah in my bed instead. Time stood still. It was as if day had turned into a thousand midnights. Darkness engulfed me and turned into furious flames of rage. When I confronted my father-in-law, he explained it wasn't their custom to give the younger in marriage before the elder. I could have Rachel after the week of completing my nuptials with Leah *if* I would agree to work for Laban another seven years. What could I do but agree? I lived to be with Rachel. Leah was nice enough, and she had nice eyes, although they were weak. Rachel was stunningly beautiful. It was her image I awakened to every morning. I was haunted by her beauty.

It wasn't fair to Leah, I know. She loved me and tried so hard, but she wasn't Rachel. The two women were as different as night and day. I could only see Rachel no matter what Leah did for me. After the seven days of nuptials with Leah, I took Rachel as my second bride and my joy returned. However, the reality of having to share my affections took a toll on them. If it had been acceptable, I would have lavished all my love on Rachel. But that would not have been right or kind.

Ironically, it was Leah who gave me the joy of children. Rachel was barren. Her barrenness marred her beauty with insecurity and jealousy. My sweet bride turned into a demanding one. At one point she even threatened me, saying, "Give me children, or I'll die!"[2] Was I in the place of God? Was it in my power to open her womb? I had sacrificed years of my life for her, and yet it was not enough. My love was not enough. This hurt me deeply, and yet I still loved her. She asked me to sleep with her maid so she could have children through her, and I complied. I would have done anything to make her happy. Rachel's servant Bilhah gave birth to two sons before my Rachel finally conceived. When Rachel's child was born, there could not have been a happier woman on the face of the earth.

Leah, who by now had given birth to our six sons and daughter, Dinah, had long relinquished the idea that I would love her the way I loved Rachel. She found solace in our children. I prayed Rachel's child would bring peace back to my household, and he did for a short time. The moment Rachel gave birth she was asking God for another child. I wondered what would truly satisfy her.

With my family growing at such a steady rate, I decided it was time for us to set off on our own. But Laban, my father-in-law, had other ideas. I'd made a bargain with him concerning my earnings, and he resorted to trickery to cheat me out of what was mine. Thankfully God intervened on my behalf. In the end I was a wealthy man.

On the day we left, Laban was furious and pursued us. He accused me of stealing his gods, his household idols. I had no idea what he was talking about, so I declared that if he found them whoever had stolen them would be put to death. Much later, when I found out that Rachel had stolen them, I was horrified that I'd given such an oath. I don't know why Rachel felt the need to cling to them when the God of my father, the God of Abraham, had proven Himself to us again and again. Perhaps she blamed God for withholding children from her. Or for making her share me with her sister. I don't know. Later I often wondered, "Did my words cut her life short?"

Rachel was so happy to discover that she was with child again. Perhaps our journey proved too much for her delicate condition. She died in childbirth. Her state of mind was apparent as she voiced her sorrow by naming our child Ben-Oni, "son of my trouble." I changed his name to Benjamin for his sake.[3] It wasn't fair for him to bear Rachel's sadness. I could make no sense of Rachel's motive. I felt I had failed her in some way. It wasn't important to me if she had children or not. I loved her from the moment I saw her. My only thoughts were of what I could give to her. I never felt like I'd given her enough.

Ironically, the one to whom I gave the least of myself gave me the most. It was Leah who was with me to the end. Unloved, she'd chosen to focus her attention on God and her children. The contest between Rachel and Leah over my affections cost our children dearly. It left scars on their hearts that I couldn't heal. Perhaps I transferred my longings for Rachel to my son Joseph. This caused further problems between him and his siblings.

In retrospect, it was Rachel's beauty that captured me, but there are some things beauty can't do. Physical beauty fades. Character stands the test of time and helps us make wise choices in relationships that build up our partners and our offspring. So be mindful. Never rely on beauty alone to keep your relationship intact. Your inner qualities will endure. Rachel was beautiful, but I would have preferred she be happy. This I realized too late.

Still regretful,

Jacob

Man to Woman

When it comes to attraction, men are primarily moved by what they see. Sometimes this blinds them to important essentials when it comes to women. When a man decides he loves a woman, there is really little that will deter him from pursuing her. He will live or die for her. He will sell all he has for her. When he has won her heart, nothing frustrates him more than feeling that his love isn't enough to keep her happy. When he's held responsible for things that are beyond his control, he questions his manhood.

A man lives to be his woman's hero. He wants to perform great feats for her. When he feels incapable of making her happy, he may shut down, abdicate his duties altogether, or turn to another source that will make him feel whole and on top of his game. This alternative may be work, other women, or a vice in which he finds temporary peace and satisfaction.

The things that are important to a woman may not be so important to a man. While she may think it's important to have children, he may not have that in mind. A man chooses his woman based on the image he has in mind of what he wants in a wife. How she looks, how she carries herself, how she makes him feel are important. Once he's acquired his prize, he is happy and sets about doing whatever he has to do to maintain her respect and honor. If he feels like a failure on any level within his love relationship, it affects everything in his life. He'll seek solace in something or someone who doesn't demand something he can't give. In this way, many women give their men to other women. Generally speaking, I believe the "other woman" doesn't *take* a man away from his wife, as much as she gets a man who has grown weary of his masculinity not being affirmed. This doesn't justify a man's adultery, but it exposes a general root problem in many cases. (In some cases, a man just has an unfaithful spirit.)

The same can be said for women. If they aren't getting the emotional support they need from their husbands, they may be easy prey for men who pay them more attention. But bottom line, beauty alone is not the answer to healthy and happy relationships.

After beauty, a man seeks peace, honor, and a general sense of fulfillment with his partner. What fulfills him most is the knowledge that he fulfills her expectations. He wants to be king in her eyes based on what he accomplishes for her sake. The absence of these things can mar what he once treasured in his mate and strangle the relationship in many ways. The power of receiving a woman's honor and pleasure is essential to keeping his love and romance fresh. A wise woman builds her house; the foolish woman tears her house down with her own hands and, usually, through her words.

The Truth of the Matter

Men are simple; women are complicated. According to popular culture, a man will sell the world for the good thing he's found. Jacob practically did that, and it still wasn't enough for Rachel. Jacob believed he'd proven his love for Rachel by working for her hand in marriage for seven years. He didn't love her because of the children she could bear for him. He loved Rachel for who she was and for her beauty. Perhaps that was hard for her to conceive of. Many women find it hard to receive love. They feel they are unworthy of it even though they desire it.

Perhaps Rachel got caught up in comparing herself to her sister. Who can say? She did miss some serious cues that probably had great impact on her relationship with Jacob. Definitely communication was broken. He was unaware of her dabbling with other gods. His careless declaration regarding the person in possession of Laban's gods could have cost Rachel her life. If he'd even suspected the person was Rachel, I'm sure he would never have uttered those words!

The things that matter to women are simply not the same things that matter to men. What we produce doesn't matter to our men. They fell in love with *us*. Our insecurities can create competitions in our minds that don't exist. This is wearisome to men. They don't know what to do with our insecurities because they don't understand them. Our insecurities must be settled between God and us. Leah finally got the message after giving birth to her son Judah (whose name means "praise"). She realized she was fighting a losing battle in trying to win Jacob's love. She decided to focus her attention on God. She stopped contending for Jacob's affection and found her solace, love, and fulfillment in God. She continued to be fruitful, and after Rachel died she had Jacob to herself. Rachel was in continual contention until the day she died, yet she was the one who was truly loved by Jacob. Learning to rest in our relationships without expectations that may or may not be possible will bring us peace. Asking a man to feel responsible for things beyond his control is like telling him he isn't a real man.

Let's remember that God is ultimately in control. It is to Him that we must take our deepest desires, our questions, and our struggles. Though men are tough on the outside, they remain very sensitive to us. What we do and say, as well as our personal opinions of them, matter greatly and can affect their views of themselves.

The greatest way to celebrate the men in our lives is to celebrate who God created us to be.

Matters of the Heart

1. What things affect your self-esteem or your sense of self-worth?

2. In what ways have you held your partner responsible for your life? For your dreams and desires? For your sense of well-being?

3. What instances cause you to question your desirability as a woman?

4. What do you need to do to build confidence in being the woman God created you to be?

How to Win Respect

My dear,

My life was filled with many adventures, though at the time it didn't feel as such. In retrospect, I can see the hand of the Lord with me in all the things I endured. My mother, Rachel, died when I was very young, but my father, Jacob, made sure I felt no loss of love. It was safe to say that I was his favorite, and this did not rest well with my siblings. I didn't realize the depth of their jealousy initially. Yes, they said things—little hurtful jabs that I didn't allow to penetrate my heart. Perhaps I was naïve. I would never wish evil upon them, so it was difficult for me to conceive of them doing that toward me.

One night I had a dream. Oh, what a dream it was! The sheaf of grain I was binding rose and stood upright, while my brothers' sheaves gathered around mine and bowed down to it.[1] I told my father and brothers about this, but they didn't seem pleased.

Then I had another dream that I again shared with them. I told them the sun and the moon bowed to me, and eleven stars followed suit.[2] My father rebuked me, and my brothers were livid. I admit

I missed the warning signs and was oblivious to being in danger. Imagine my shock at what transpired next.

My father sent me to check on my brothers where they were shepherding our flocks. When I approached, they grabbed me and threw me into a dry well. At first I thought it to be just a joke. Their way of chastising me for having, as they put it, lofty visions of grandeur. But it turned into a nightmare. Later my brothers, all except Reuben, pulled me out of the well and sold me off as a common slave. They watched me being taken away by Midianite traders. Can you imagine? They stood there and stared as I pleaded with them. They were as still and as quiet as stones when I was led away. I called out for Reuben, but evidently he couldn't hear me. I called out to anyone who would listen, but my cries fell on deaf ears...or so I thought.

Then I was sold again when we got to Egypt. To Potiphar, the captain of the guard for the Pharaoh.[3] I was confident that God was still with me. Potiphar was a man of stature who had no time for cruelty though he was a man of war. He took notice of my conscientious work. I ran his household with the same precision of the military because that was what he wanted. Potiphar spent many days away, coming and going, so he promoted me and placed me over all his staff. He entrusted everything he owned into my care because he saw that God was with me.

I thanked God for His faithfulness. Instead of giving me a cruel master to add insult to the injury of being sold by my own brothers, He had elevated me even in the midst of hardship. I saw His hand in this. It was a blessing I refused to deny.

But then it changed. Potiphar's wife was lonely and bored. I first noticed her watching me from across the room. I pretended not to notice the intensity of her stare. I kept my distance, but she was always finding excuses to call me into her presence. These meetings I kept as short as possible without being disrespectful. Still she persisted in trying to catch my attention. Finally, as if she was a volcano erupting and could contain herself no longer, she invited me to come and lie with her. I was shocked. Forward Egyptian women were something else! I couldn't imagine a Hebrew woman in a similar position doing such a thing. It simply wasn't done.

I decided I would reason with her. I didn't want to offend her or make her feel rejected, but I also couldn't do what she asked. As I stand before God I couldn't sin against Him in light of His mercy. I tried to get Potiphar's wife to think rationally about what she was proposing. Did she not see that she would ruin her standing if she became involved with me? Familiarity breeds contempt. If I slept with her, I would not see her in the same way. This would lead to me despising her authority. How could I take orders from someone I slept with? I tried to get her to see the light. She would be a far better master if the boundary lines were drawn. To blur the line with intimacy would cause irresolvable issues. Once we crossed the line, there would be no turning back.[4]

For me the situation was clear. What she proposed was a sin against God. It wasn't a matter of what would happen should I be caught. It was a matter of how God would feel. I didn't want to grieve Him. He was all I had. I realized Egyptian society didn't have the same moral code my culture did. For her, this dalliance was nothing. No big deal. But for me it was monumental. I felt disappointed. I also didn't want to violate the trust Potiphar had placed in me. I wanted to keep his wife in high esteem, but she was making it difficult for me to do so.

I decided it would be best for both of our sakes for me to keep my distance. It was never my intent to make her feel rejected, and yet she took my avoidance to heart. It seemed to incense her even more. When she called for some kind of service, I sent others to do her bidding. One day I noticed the house was empty. All the servants were gone. The woman requested my presence, and I had no choice but to answer her summons. When I went to her, she grabbed me and pressed me passionately to sleep with her.

She was beautiful. I was tempted in my flesh, but my spirit reminded me of my commitment to God and to Potiphar. I turned and fled. I could feel my cloak slipping off me, but I dared not look back. I ran for my life. I ran for her chastity. I ran to secure my relationship with God.

Potiphar's wife screamed in rage. When her husband got home, she accused me of rape, using the garment left behind as evidence against me. The look in Potiphar's eyes was chilling. He burned with anger and had me thrown into prison.

While I sat there considering my fate, the Lord extended His kindness and gave me favor with the jailer. But I still wondered how it had come to this. Why would a woman want to throw her respectability away? Why would she destroy her relationship with her husband for a moment of passion? I could never be a serious consideration or tolerate being a slave boy held for sport. How could I respect her after being forced to view her nakedness and know her in such an intimate fashion? It was not possible, but these were things she could not, would not consider. Her anger confused me. Shouldn't she have been relieved that I didn't take advantage of her weakness? My resistance seemed to have the opposite effect.

And so in prison I sat.

And God was with me. I was there for some time before I met the Pharaoh's wine steward and baker. They were troubled by dreams, but God gave me the discernment to interpret for them. They thanked me profusely when they were released from jail. I asked them to remember me and explain my plight to the Pharaoh. Though the interpretation I gave them of their dreams came to pass, after two years of waiting it was clear they'd forgotten about me. Through God's miraculous power, presence, and grace, one day I was taken out of the prison and appointed as the right-hand man of the Pharaoh of Egypt.

I outranked even Potiphar! I saw his wife one day in court. She averted her eyes for fear of my reprisal. But I felt no anger...only pity. I was free of her deceit. And that's the point I want to make to you today. You never know where life will lead you or who you will encounter on your path. It behooves you to build a solid foundation based on God and His principles that can never be misconstrued or leave you in danger of shame and regret. Take the path of honor always.

Respectfully,

Joseph

Man to Woman

Today's culture has deceived many women into a sense of false liberation. What women need to know is that forwardness and loosened moral codes are setups for becoming disrespected. When women become the aggressors in romantic relationships, they undermine the very things God put in place to make them treasured and protected vessels. What's good for the goose is not good for the gander.

When women are in leadership, it is even more important that they maintain high moral principles at all times. To mix business with pleasure is a slippery slope that may compromise the people involved and render them powerless and fruitless in their endeavors.

It confuses matters and muddies the playing field. In the end, one person in the equation may feel used, rejected, or sullied.

We all have needs, but they must be kept in the right perspective. A woman erodes the foundation of the very things she demands whenever she puts herself in an unethical position. To make romantic advances toward a man, especially in the marketplace, is an open invitation to be insulted and hurt. This can lead nowhere and isn't conducive to success or wholeness.

And when adultery enters the picture, the losses are even greater. Loss of family, loss of standing in the work arena, and loss of friends are demoralizing. If there is any deception within you that implies something meaningful can come out of something that started on the wrong foundation, cast it off right away. Men do not love women they don't respect.

The Truth of the Matter

Life happens. Especially when voids are left open to fester in our lives. Desire and need can push us over the edge and prod us to do things we wouldn't do under normal circumstances. Perhaps Potiphar stayed away from home too long, leaving his wife with too much time to consider other options. Perhaps she was moved and fascinated by how handsome Joseph was. We don't know the underlying issues of why Joseph caught the fancy of Potiphar's wife. What we do know is that she was relentless in her pursuit of him.

Jewish historian Josephus paints the scenario of Joseph going to great lengths to try to get his master's wife to see things rationally. He informs her that should he submit to dalliances with her, the familiarity between them would destroy their working relationship. He would no longer be able to respect or submit to her. He urged her to maintain her position as an honored mistress of the house by keeping their relationship pure. She would not be swayed from her pursuit. He then began avoiding her, which I am sure incensed her even more. Now pride entered the picture in the face of rejection. Tensions obviously mounted in the midst of this cat-and-mouse game that exploded into a major disaster.

For those of us looking at this story from the sidelines the outcome was no surprise. Rejection usually leads to retaliation when the rejected becomes embittered.

The rest of the story is history. Can you imagine how Potiphar's wife felt when she got the news that Joseph had been promoted to the position of right-hand man to Pharaoh? The thoughts that must have gone through her head! Would he retaliate now that he was in power? How would she face him should their paths ever cross?

The moment of facing our comeuppance and reaping what we've sown is inevitable. Wielding power over others because we can is never right. If we want respect, we must give it. For this reason, we all need to reflect on the effects we want to have on others.

Determine the light you want to be seen in, and then set personal boundaries that ensure your position. When you walk in purity, God will always guard your reputation. The job of guarding your heart belongs to you; however, God is able to keep your heart from exposure to things that would injure it if you submit to Him.

Matters of the Heart

1. What do your relationships in the marketplace look like?

2. How do you handle temptation when you're in a needy place?

3. What measures do you need to put in place to avoid compromising your standards?

A Woman's Strength

My dear,

Suffice it to say, I've always been an admirer of women. I find their strength admirable and needed in a man's world. Perhaps I've drawn this conclusion because, in my opinion, I was led by the best. During my time, Deborah was judge over Israel.[1] She wore her position with a grace that inspired men to acknowledge her authority and submit. She was feminine. She didn't deny that, and she never walked outside the bounds of femininity though she held such a high office.

Deborah was the wife of Lappidoth, and everyone knew her marriage was sacred and dear to her. It was noted that we could not...should not...ignore her married status. Her husband was very much a part of who she was. He was well spoken of in the gates because of her. She was a woman of great virtue. She was also a prophet. This gave her insights into the heart of God and helped her rule His people accordingly. She was uncompromising of His standards, and those who stood before her knew they were hearing from God.

This judge of Israel was formidable because she was wise. She wore wisdom like a cloak. Those who sought her counsel were made the richer by the knowledge she shared. She had ways of dispensing truth and judging matters so they were uncontested. Many sought her out because they were sure the outcome would be just.

Though she was a judge, she was also a mother. Yes, she was heralded as a mother in Israel. Tender, strong, nurturing, principled, kind but firm. Her instruction brought life to all who received it. Her counsel wasn't ignored. To do so would mean the people had chosen the path of fools. When she summoned people, they arrived in anticipation of receiving a word that would change their lives and redirect their course.

The day she called me to appear before her was like that. She'd seated herself under the palms and was enjoying the breeze and the constant flow of those who came seeking her counsel and asking for matters to be settled. When it was my turn, her eyes were penetrating as she challenged my heart. She made it clear that God had called me to go out in battle against Sisera, an enemy of the people of Israel. Though she said that God assured us of the victory, my heart was shaken by fear as I thought of the prospect of facing the fierce army and even fiercer general.

I dared not disobey God, but I felt I could not move forward on my own. A glint of disappointment flashed in her eyes when I proposed that she go with me to the battlefield. However, she didn't berate me. She said she would go, but because I wouldn't go alone, a woman would be given the glory for the battle being won.[2] She gave me the choice, and I bowed to what she declared. For me, it wasn't important who got credit for winning the battle; I just wanted the battle to be won. When Deborah consented to go with me, I summoned Naphtali and Zebulun to go into battle too. We took ten companies of men and headed to Kadesh.

Heber the Kenite told Sisera that I had gone to Mount Tabor. Sisera then rounded up 900 iron chariots along with 100,000 troops. Their appearance was a fearful sight, and yet Deborah seemed unmoved. She motioned to me saying, "Charge! This very day GOD has given you victory over Sisera. Isn't God marching before you?"[3] That was all I needed to hear!

I charged down the slopes of Mount Tabor. What Deborah had said was true. God routed Sisera's troops. We chased and overtook them all. Their defeat was so great that Sisera dismounted his horse and ran for safety. Little did he know he was running toward his defeat. He sought refuge in the tent of Jael. She encouraged him to rest and then, while he was sleeping, drove a tent peg through his skull.

When I reached him, he was dead.

Oh, how we rejoiced! No one sought to take credit for the victory. Truly, it was an act of God. He fought the battle for us. The stars in the sky rallied behind us sending torrential rains to throw the enemy into confusion and wash them away.[4] We were only partners with God in the fight. He gave us the victory. This we knew well. God literally gave Sisera over to Jael for destruction.

There was no room for competition. The victory belonged to us all. Deborah and I sang a victory song together. She, a mother of Israel, rose up and called us to action. She went with us to the battlefield, and then she urged us forward. Backed by her encouragement, we found the courage to fight. She never lost her femininity while inspiring us to be the men God had called us to be. There was no resentment of her leadership because she allowed us our dignity. We *wanted* to fight for her, for God, for our people. What we lacked in zeal and confidence, her presence and example filled in. She was God's instrument in that hour to make sure His agenda was carried out. Deborah's influence was the catalyst to us carrying out God's mission.

If it hadn't been for her words of encouragement and her

willingness to see the battle through with us, we may not have gone. But her presence meant everything. She was the rallying cry and the resounding force behind us. While many of the tribes of Israel didn't show up to fight, it made no difference. God used what He had—a faithful few in the face of a fierce enemy. Perhaps He chose to honor Deborah for her unwavering trust in Him and His Word, thus securing our victory.

I was honored to be part of the battle. And though the highest honor went to a woman, to Jael, I felt no shame. Deborah graciously acknowledged and praised me for my role in winning the war. This humbled me. I couldn't have done it without her, and yet she didn't belittle me for refusing to go without her. She was gracious and affirming, nurturing her people to greatness and freedom.

After the battle we had peace for forty years.

They say behind every great man is a great woman. I will take it one step further: Behind every great and peaceful nation is a woman wielding her power and influence well.

Forever in her service,

Barak

Man to Woman

In today's world, it is said that men are intimidated by powerful women. I think that's an excuse for some women who have ascended corporate ladders to behave badly. Men know that women are powerful. Their mothers teach them that. What men don't like are women who wield their power and announce it to the world. When a woman's power becomes about her and not about the partnership or the job at hand, she becomes unattractive. In other words, she should let her work speak for itself.

The most powerful gift a woman has is the gift of influence. She can help a man become accomplished and powerful. However, he doesn't want to feel that he is being manipulated or "made." A man responds to a woman's affirmation. To her validation of him as a man. Her faith in him makes him want to scale the highest heights to earn her admiration and respect.

When she puts him in constant remembrance of her own achievements, he finds it belittling, as if she is comparing him to herself and he is coming up short. He doesn't want to be compared to a woman, especially if his achievements don't match or surpass hers. It attacks his masculinity, the core of who he is supposed to be as a man. He strives to be provider and protector. The one who adds to a woman's world and contributes to her well-being. If he feels he is failing in these areas, he'll move on to another situation where he can feel he's succeeding.

A man is willing to stand behind, support, and celebrate a powerful woman only if that woman allows him to feel powerful too. If he isn't financially successful, he needs to feel as if his presence makes a difference. That he is needed in some capacity that affirms his masculinity. He willingly follows a woman into battle if he knows she will allow him to get the spoils for her.

My dear, if you are successful, if you are powerful, let those virtues speak for themselves. There is no need for you to announce them. The fruit of your works will reveal themselves appropriately in a way that allows everyone to celebrate the successes.

The Truth of the Matter

No one likes people who are full of themselves. Male or female, the ones who celebrate themselves don't leave room for others to celebrate with them. Tooting our own horns is not living graciously. What made Deborah so attractive and effective in leading and working with powerful men was her ability to maintain who she was as a woman. Even the way she approached Barak left her out of the equation. She didn't render her opinion about what he was supposed to be doing. Instead, she put him in remembrance of what God expected of him.

Perhaps this is the key to success. Not to vaunt our expectations of the men in our lives, but rather to encourage them to do what God created them to do. This is empowering. When we do this without judgment, criticism, or demands, men will rise to the occasion. This position also frees them to admit when they need help from us.

When Barak told Deborah he wanted her to go with him into battle, she didn't put him down for asking. She did let him know he was capable of winning the battle without her. She was willing to go; however, if she went Barak wouldn't get full credit for the victory. I believe her approach put things in perspective for him so that he could see that was *not* what was important. Winning the battle was the issue no matter who got the credit. Deborah was a team player. Men know when we're on their team. When we are at their side. When we have their back. Our support can make or break them. We can work to their advantage or be distractions that hinder them from moving forward.

How you approach your relationship or the business at hand is up to you. Is it more important to celebrate yourself and your achievements or to allow your works to attract praise?

God created women to be powerful and to be used powerfully by Him. However, there is a best way to go about it. Deborah's example of gracious leadership serves to let us know it is not the position of a woman but the *dis*position that makes the difference in our relationships. It's not who gets the credit for winning the war; it is winning the war that matters.

As we partner together to win victories for the home team, both men and women are affirmed and validated as major contributors. This is evident in the song Deborah and Barak sang together after the victory. Everyone who participated was celebrated![5] As we walk through life together, partnerships are important. Few victories are won alone. When we walk in that understanding, our relationships become different. Success is no longer about one person but about who we are as a couple, unit, or team. This is when we bear the most fruit—fruit that lasts and love that flourishes.

The Heart of the Matter

1. How do you handle your personal successes? Does it infringe on your relationships with men?

2. How do you handle the shortcomings of the men in your life?

3. How can you influence the men in your life to greater victories?

The Price of Control

My dear,

One thing I've learned in this life is when a woman makes up her mind about something, she'll make it happen! But "at what price" becomes the question. Take my wife, for instance. Jezebel was beautiful, charismatic, and powerful. I was drawn to her in a way that can't be explained. She exuded sexuality. Everyone who met her was seduced by her in some form. She was downright intoxicating, and she never took no for an answer. Before a person knew it, he was drawn into her web, and her wish became his command.

When I married her, Jezebel brought along her worship of the pagan gods Baal and Asherah. She also brought the prophets who served those gods.[1] She housed them and fed them. She gave herself totally to the worship of her idols. Though I knew it was wrong, I felt compelled to follow suit.

I built a grove for her god Asherah and a place of worship in Samaria for Baal. Jezebel was ardent in her beliefs, and soon the people followed her by worshipping Baal and bowing before her idols. She was delighted, and I was happy that she was happy.

Once these customs were established, Jezebel set her sights on exterminating all of the prophets of God, along with anyone who rejected her brand of worship. I didn't want to deny her pleasure. Soon the land was silent as the prophets of God who weren't killed went into hiding.[2]

Then Elijah showed up, calling for a showdown between Baal, Asherah, and the Lord at Mt. Carmel. I remember the day vividly. Elijah's God won. When my wife heard what Elijah had done, her beautiful face was contorted, so great was her rage. The heat of her anger filled the room as she paced back and forth spewing curses and vile threats against Elijah. *How dare he make a mockery of my gods!* She couldn't stop saying it. She resolved to kill him. She would not rest until she did.

I was afraid for her, but again I said nothing. After all, this man called down fire from heaven! The proof that his God was mightier than Baal couldn't be denied. At Mt. Carmel, Jezebel's prophets had abased themselves and called out to Baal most of the day with no results. Then Elijah had the people pour water over his altar, including the wood, several times. He called to God, and God sent fire from heaven that consumed everything—including the water![3] How could there be any question which God was superior? Those gathered decided the proof was in the miracle. They conceded by rounding up all the false prophets and slaughtering them, as commanded by Elijah.

I couldn't understand why Jezebel wanted to continually contend with Elijah and defy his God. This same prophet decreed a drought for three years, and that happened. Truly his God was at work. But my darling wife wouldn't be swayed or deterred. She was bound to Baal and would fight to the bitter end for him no matter the cost.

Jezebel issued her edict that she would have the head of Elijah, and I was shocked to learn that this powerful prophet fled and went into hiding. This man who had shut the heavens from giving rain and called down fire feared her threats. All the more reason to marvel at her power. Yes, I too was seduced by her. Though I knew what she did was wrong, I was too caught up to insist on principle. She influenced me into doing things I wouldn't do of my own volition. I couldn't bear the thought of garnering her displeasure. I would do anything that made her happy, even sacrificing my own beliefs.

My wife was something! Once I spotted a vineyard next to the palace that I wanted, but its owner, Naboth, wouldn't sell it to me.[4] He kept going on about it being his family's inheritance. I was so upset he couldn't be bribed that I took to my bed depressed. Jezebel noticed my foul mood and questioned me. I told her about my interaction with Naboth. The look of disgust on her face made my heart drop to my stomach. I felt like a rodent so repulsive she couldn't mask how she felt.

"What is wrong with you?" she demanded. "Are you king or not?" Those words rang in my ears. And then she assured me she would take care of it. I didn't know what that meant at the time, so imagine my shock when it was relayed to me that Naboth was dead. Jezebel told me, "Get up and take possession of the vineyard of Naboth the Jezreelite that he refused to sell you. He is no longer alive, but dead."

I wondered how she'd manipulated key people on the council to get Naboth discredited and stoned to death. What else was she capable of? Would she be my demise? I dared not allow my thoughts to wander down that trail. Jezebel was so elated to tell me the field was now mine that I dared not dampen her joy by questioning how she brought it about. So I put on a happy face, conveyed the right amount of gratefulness, and went to take possession of the vineyard. But inside I felt a sense of dread.

Sure enough God was not amused. Guess who found me in

Naboth's field? Elijah himself. He said God had spoken against me because of Naboth's murder. The prophet said dogs would lick up my blood and my descendants would be wiped out. He added that dogs would also devour Jezebel.

What could I say? I knew I was in the wrong. I knew my reputation for being evil was justified. I can't explain my boldness in defying God. Perhaps I was weak and driven by my love for Jezebel and her wicked ways. She was part of me; she was in my blood. And now I would pay for my ardor. My heart was cut to the quick at the words of Elijah.

I bowed in repentance. Only this stayed the hand of God against me, but my punishment would fall on the next generation. My sons and daughters would suffer for what Jezebel and I had done. At the time I hadn't looked to the future to see what my sins might cost my family. I thought only of my wife and me. I concede that Jezebel too thought only of us. She was a master at manipulation, and I gave in willingly.

I've wondered in retrospect what life would have been like if I'd not given in to her whims. I let her power over me be greater than my fear of God. That is my greatest regret. The blame isn't all on her, yet I point my finger at the part she played. She took advantage of my emotions as only a woman can do. She swayed me to wrong.

I pray that you, my dear, will use your influence in more fruitful ways that lead to life and not to death. And not just for yourself, but for future generations too. One person affects many. Remember that in those times when you feel drawn away from the right path to follow your own fancy. It's a matter of life and death.

In hindsight comes wisdom,

Ahab

Man to Woman

A man lives to be his woman's hero and king. He'll do whatever he needs to in order to see the light of admiration in her eyes. He longs for her praise. The deepest and most hurtful wounds a man can suffer aren't physical but come from the sting of a woman's tongue. Words of disrespect and criticism cut deeply into his being. Yes, a man will live or die for the praise of his woman. He'll go against the grain of his own soul to win and keep her love.

This is the influence of a woman. The husband may be the head in a marriage, but the wife is the neck that turns the head to the left or to the right.[5] A woman has the capacity to change a man for the better or for the worse. Her inspiration or the things she demands may become the pressure he allows to make his character shine or shatter. She was created by God to be a helper for him. God gave her the powerful gift of influence that she can wield for good or bad.

As strong as your man is, he is vulnerable when it comes to you. Your opinion of him alters who he believes he is. You get to the heart of his masculinity. You can build him up so he feels he's sitting on top of the world, or you can tear him down so he feels he's the most worthless creature on the face of the earth. Therefore, be careful. Consider the weight of your opinions and observances. Speak in ways that inspire your man to be the person God created him to be—a man of integrity and sound character.

The Truth of the Matter

We can all be selfish, but we were not created to live in a vacuum and pursue only our interests. We were created to be part of a team who can win battles for God and the advancement of His kingdom. All aspects of relational living, especially marriage, are designed to give us a foretaste of what heaven will be like. A oneness of spirit that promotes God's agenda on the earth as well as in heaven. This means we must focus on producing good fruit that will, to the glory of God, remain as a legacy that continues to bless others long after we've departed. When we get caught up in selfish agendas, we abandon God's plan of righteous living. The virtuous woman becomes not so virtuous, and her husband becomes not so well-spoken of at the city gates. He may also have need for dishonest gain because of the demands he tries to meet for his wife.

A woman needs to consider how she affects her man and what that means in light of God. To encourage your man to unrighteousness affects the two of you *and* the generations to come. The decisions you make today won't stop here. They'll carry the weight of results into tomorrow. The sons and daughters of Ahab suffered the consequences for Ahab's offenses. Jezebel's daughter, Athaliah, for instance, inherited her mom's evil nature and killed her own grandchildren.[6]

We set the atmosphere in our homes as well as influence family dynamics. We need to be mindful to always use our influence in positive ways. Manipulation is witchcraft in the eyes of God.[7] God will hold you accountable for your behavior and for the behavior of others you've led astray.

It's easy to believe that strong opinions are a function of being a strong woman, especially for those who are single and live on their own. But when in a romantic relationship, it's important to allow your man to be a man. To take the lead. To make decisions corporately with you that benefit you both. Never selfishly resort to exercising wiles to cause him to go against what he knows is right. Be an example of walking in agreement and respecting authority to your children. Remember, you are building a legacy in your home as well as in the marketplace. Getting your way today may cause your undoing tomorrow.

The Heart of the Matter

1. What is your usual response if someone you love, whether a spouse or someone else, doesn't live up to your wishes?

2. How do you respond when someone thwarts your desires?

3. How do you go about making the things you're passionate about happen?

4. What do you need to surrender to align yourself with God's desires and release control to Him?

The Importance of Wisdom

My dear,

If you want a man to adore you and honor you, let me suggest how you can go about it. As much time as you spend on your outer image, there is a deeper beauty that can't be seen with human eyes but is detectable by the heart. It may appear to be unassuming at first, but it is powerful and lasting It will knit the heart of a man to you and encourage him to love you in a way you never dreamed possible.

When a man is young, he gets swept away by a woman's outer body. But once he has lived a while and gone through some life storms, he realizes he wants beauty that is more than skin deep. People need more than good looks to make it through life successfully. What attribute am I referring to? Wisdom. We need wisdom. Wisdom leads to a full life, success, and honor.

Michal, my first wife, was beautiful. She was the daughter of King Saul, and I fought for the right to wed her.[1] She was a fitting prize. She loved me so much that she betrayed her father to save my life. With her help, I escaped Saul's murderous rage and went on the run with a band of followers who supported me. It was a hard life. My men and I lived off the resources of the land. Those who were in our path as we escaped Saul's men were gracious, offering what they could to assist us. We, in turn, offered protection for them, their families, their flocks, and their belongings.

One day we found it reasonable to request provisions from a wealthy landowner named Nabal.[2] After all, we'd been protecting all that was his. However, he proved to be surly and insolent. He chose to insult my men and me. I was furious and quite ready to wipe out all the men in his household. As I rallied my forces to do just that, I was interrupted by an amazing woman.

This woman came riding up on a donkey. She said her name was Abigail, and she was Nabal's wife. Though she was pleasant to look upon, I was more intrigued by her humble demeanor and what she had to say. She came with provisions that she generously offered to us. She apologized for the behavior of her husband. She acknowledged that his actions had been foolish and that, though it was a part of his character, she wouldn't justify his behavior. And she stood in the gap for him by asking for forgiveness and mercy.

And then she said something that struck me. She prophesied. She reminded me of the call on my life and reasoned with me that I didn't need to have unnecessary blood on my hands. I marveled that she saw my future and spoke so wisely. What a rare woman! This woman saw what God saw in me and pointed her finger toward it. "Keep focused," she said. "Don't get distracted. Don't allow my husband's foolishness to bring out the fool in you. You will be king!" So firm was her belief that she asked me to remember her when I came into my kingdom.

I thanked her and praised God for sending Abigail out to meet me. I accepted her gift of provisions and said, "Go home in peace."

After she left, I wondered how such a foolish man had married such a wise woman. I was sure she hadn't consulted her husband before she set off from home to appease me. She'd made the quick decision to secure her husband's holdings despite his recklessness and the danger he'd placed their household in. She defended him even though she acknowledged his faults. I hoped his anger wouldn't burn against her once he discovered what she'd done. A man that foolish might not see what her prudence had accomplished.

Then I heard that Nabal died within days of my interaction with Abigail. I felt that God had spared her because she was a woman in tune with Him. He'd used her to keep me from doing what I should not have considered. Abigail intervened on my behalf as well as hers. While Nabal probably didn't understand the quality of woman she was, I saw it clearly. I sent for Abigail, asking her to be my wife. In my mind I knew I'd be better for having this woman by my side. I needed wisdom beside me in those moments that come for every man when he doesn't think clearly because the pressures of life have taken their toll. Yes, I needed her. I wanted her. I loved her for the man she allowed me to be.

Ah, but then I had another wife who would have done well to learn from Abigail. Michal, for all her beauty and passion, wasn't so wise. She never understood the calling on my life or my devotion to God. Perhaps she was too embittered to see or care because of all that had transpired when I fled from her father's wrath. I couldn't take her with me because it would have further enraged her father. He would have used her being with me as an excuse to incite people against me. I'm sure he would have accused me of kidnapping and then played the aggrieved father role to the hilt. I couldn't take that chance, so I had to leave her behind.

Much later, after I'd gotten the throne, I learned that Saul had given Michal in marriage to another man. But she was still my wife. I sent for her. I heard that her husband Paltiel had followed her, weeping, until they turned him back. This was the drama that followed Michal back to my home.

During this time, the Ark of the Covenant was in Baalah in Judah. I gathered 30,000 soldiers and went to get it back. I was so elated that, upon its entrance into my city, I danced in front of it with all my might. I danced and danced until I danced myself right out of my outer garments.

I was excited about sharing this blessing with Michal. Yes, I intended to bless her and all within my household. But when I returned home, what met me at the door dampened my spirit and made my heart cold. Michal berated me for dancing in the street. She basically scolded me for not maintaining the "posture of a king" and dancing out of my garments so I was clad only in a linen ephod before the people.[3] She killed the joy of the moment and pierced my heart. Something inside me shut down that day. She lost my heart; she lost my love. I told her the same maids she was so worried about seeing me scantily clad would continue to hold me in honor.

Michal was such a sharp contrast to Abigail, who saw my calling, understood it, believed it, and helped me stay focused on the end result rather than on the madness between start and finish. Michal missed the point of Who I was all about. A man needs a woman's foresight and encouragement. These wisdom qualities last beyond physical beauty and will stand the test of time. This is the attraction of wisdom. It never loses its appeal.

Insightfully yours,

David

Man to Woman

Men understand that they need women in their lives. Not just any women, but women who are good for them. In my experience, for the most part mothers don't prepare their sons for being self-sufficient. When their sons go out on their own, they look for women to help them. This sets up a catch-22. Men want women who make them feel like kings, and yet they also want to be nurtured. Men, for the most part, don't function well alone. A woman grounds a man. Helps put life in perspective. Enables him to become who God created him to be.

While men process things differently—no frills, straight to the bottom line—women have the powerful gift of discernment, which works hand-in-hand with influence. These gifts are at the height of operation when women are tuned into God. A man loves a woman in the sense that he feels he is better with her than without her. I'm not talking about a woman who constantly tells him what to do, but rather a woman who, by her demeanor and the way she couches instruction, provides inspiration in light of who she believes he is capable of becoming. To kill his spirit or derail his dreams and aspirations through harshness and criticism is the fastest way to lose the heart of a man. Because a man longs to be king in the eyes of the woman in his life, he'll strive to the utmost to live up to her expectations.

A man revels in knowing that his woman "gets" or understands him. That she too has a vision of who he is in light of what God has deposited in his spirit. He draws power from her understanding resonating with his sense of purpose. Ideally, a couple becomes coconspirators in completing God's plan. Men are driven to be fruitful, to be productive. This is part of the core of who they are. So the woman in a man's life needs to be a *facilitator* rather than an inhibitor of that inclination. As she partners with him being and doing all that he was created to do, the bonds of love will grow between them, solidifying their union.

The Truth of the Matter

Women can be just as controlling as they can be inspirational. A fine line is drawn between the two, and we must be careful not to cross it. If we travel back to the Garden of Eden, we see that woman was created to assist man in completing his God-given assignments. That being the case, the best thing a woman can do is be intimately in touch with God. In this way her ear is always open to directions she receives for the sake of her man as well as herself. When she gives encouragement or instruction to her partner, the knowledge is not coming from human opinion but from divine guidance.

A man doesn't want another mother. He wants a best friend, a sister, and a lover. He'll resent being berated or manipulated. He'll withdraw by refusing and ignoring counsel if he feels it comes from a selfish place or a desire to control. This requires a woman be sensitive not just to what she is saying but to when she is saying it. She must examine her motives and carefully place her words. A word fitly spoken is more profitable than thousands of words misplaced.

Let me be clear on what I believe our assignments are in men's lives. It is to understand what God has called him to do and then partner with him in that endeavor and assist him in achieving it. Love will grow stronger and last longer through fulfilling a purpose together rather than relying on chemistry as a bond.

Matters of the Heart

1. In what ways can you nurture and inspire the man in your life to become who God created him to be?

2. In what ways do you need to improve the way you communicate with your partner? With other men in your life?

3. What do you need to do to get a clearer understanding of how you can be instrumental in helping the man in your life be his best?

Building a Legacy

My dear,

I know you've heard about Bathsheba and me over and over through the years. I'm not going to rehearse how we became a couple. Instead, I'd rather point to a different aspect of our relationship that is often overlooked because it's not as dramatic as the beginning of our story. Suffice it to say that "beginning" is one thing, but how we finish is critical to the legacy we leave. The choices we make along the way determine how we finish—whether we crash and burn or are successful. We can figure life out on our own, or we can make sure we have the best people around us to help us make good decisions, fulfill our divine purposes, and secure our destinies. I have Bathsheba to thank for discovering this truth.

So much transpired in the years after Bathsheba and I married. I can't say I was a perfect king, but I did my best. I strove to hear from God and follow His instructions on how to lead His people. Sometimes I went off the path, and I paid the price.

One of my biggest regrets was not dealing with my son Amnon for raping his sister Tamar.[1] I confess my guilt. What had transpired between Bathsheba, Uriah, and me kept me from speaking out as I should have. I allowed my guilt and self-condemnation to silence me. I know my son Absalom resented my lack of action on Tamar's behalf. My passivity opened the door for chaos, strife, and murder. Later I could only hang my head in shame and grieve over what took place between two of my sons.

Years later, Absalom rebelled against me, openly disgracing me and leading the country in revolt against me. Instead of confronting him, I fled because I felt I had no right to correct him in light of what I'd done, along with what I had *not* done.

I loved my children—perhaps too much. Even as God defended me and restored me back to the throne, I was grieving, inconsolable over the death of Absalom. My mistakes cost me the lives of two of my sons, as well as the violation of my daughter. These things I thought of often in my old age. As I felt the life draining from my body and making me cold, I thought of what I could have done differently. Even as Abishag, the young lady who came to serve me, kept me warm, these thoughts played over and over in my mind.[2]

Imagine my dismay when Bathsheba came to tell me that my son Adonijah had set himself up as king unbeknownst to me. She reminded me that I had promised Solomon would inherit the throne and be king after I was gone to be with the Lord. She was followed by the prophet Nathan, who confirmed what she'd said. I knew with my last bit of strength that I must do something right away. So I told Bathsheba her son Solomon would be king. And then I called for Nathan the prophet, Zadok the priest, and Benaiah son of Jehoiadah and told them to go and anoint Solomon as king over Israel.[3]

I felt bad because I knew Solomon would inherit trouble. I knew his brothers would come against him since, even now, they were aligning themselves with Adonijah. But I was also sure that

Solomon was fit for the task and would know what to do when the time came. I comforted myself with the knowledge that he would have his mother to guide him after I was gone.

Bathsheba was a wise woman. From the beginning she'd seen the greatness in Solomon and had imparted knowledge that would prepare him for his position. Under her instruction he'd proven to possess great wisdom and soundness of thought. He had a way of discerning situations and knowing what to do that could only be divinely inspired. Bathsheba had given herself to his tutelage, spending great amounts of time with him and instructing him in the way that he should take, so that when he grew old he wouldn't depart from it. I had every confidence Solomon would follow my example and serve God and His people with integrity.

After Solomon was installed on the throne and taking care of all who stood against him, I instructed him on what he would need to do after I was gone to establish his reign. He listened intently, and I was sure my instructions would be followed to the letter.

I marveled at Bathsheba. I knew she'd seen this moment coming long ago and made sure she prepared our son for it. Wise mothers can see God's calling on the lives of their children and help guide them toward their destinies. Putting a sense of responsibility in their children so they are in constant remembrance of their purpose is the greatest thing mothers can do for them. In this way the children grow to be wise because they know to make every decision in light of their purpose instead of personal whims. It's critical to instill purpose and the weight of what responsibility means in the hearts of children.

For those who feel that children will find their own way, I dare to differ. It's up to the parents and responsible adults to write on the children's hearts the vision God wants them to run with. They look to us for guidance and instruction, and we must give it. Bathsheba was good at planting seeds and then standing back to watch them grow. This is one of the things she did that gained my lasting love and respect. I knew I could go in peace because she remained. She would help Solomon carry out his assignments and give him necessary guidance. With so much palace intrigue going on, he would need someone he knew he could trust.

Solomon was in good hands because his mother understood his purpose and destiny. I urge you to do the same for the children in your charge. No child was born as an accident. Each one was created with a specific purpose in God's mind. It's up to us to help them set out on the path to fulfill what was ordained for them.

As you look at your children, hold them close to your heart...but even closer to the will of God. That is part of your calling as a parent or guardian; it is part of your purpose. With this accomplished, you too can rest in peace.

Purposefully yours,

David

Man to Woman

A man feels the call to go out and provide for his family. Although this takes him away from home, home is always on his mind. The welfare of his wife and children is of great importance to him. He worries about raising their children and who they'll become. He can rest easier when he knows his wife is a woman of wisdom who will instill the right things into the hearts of their children when he isn't present. Though a husband establishes the law in their home, the wife is the one who primarily instills instruction. She is the main influencer in their children's lives. A mother's gift is the ability to see into the hearts of her children and locate their giftings. She is given glimpses of her children's futures through the eyes of God.

Though the husband is the head of the family, the woman represents the heart. She's the extension of God who nurtures and deposits dreams and visions in the children regarding where they will go and what they will do in life. Her words can plant tremendous seeds that bear incredible fruit or they can destroy the spirits of their children. What she speaks into her children's lives from an early age helps shape their character and paint visions of their future.

Children are the true legacy of any family. After parents are gone, they carry on the work. A father prays that his sons and daughters will do him proud and choose to carry on the work God desires. He wants the memory of them to live on for generations in a good light for contributing something of lasting significance to the world.

As a husband and father advances in years, some things that were once important decline in priority. He sees different aspects and qualities in his wife. His primary focus is no longer about beauty or even chemistry but more about what she brings to the party to solidify his family and root his children in ways that help them be credits and not disgraces to the family name and society. He entrusts to his wife the task of focusing their children on acquiring the wisdom that will give them firm foundations for the future.

A husband looks to his wife to partner with him in this. Few things grieve him more than when his wife, the mother of his children, doesn't establish good character and integrity with a sense of direction in each child. As his heart rests in his wife, he relies on her to give credence to what he believes. He knows his children will be set on the path of right-standing with God, equipped with great understanding of who they are and what they have to offer the world in service to God. He knows if his children have a clear vision of their purpose and calling, they will do well.

The Truth of the Matter

The story of David and Bathsheba could so easily have gone terribly wrong. Bathsheba, in sharp contrast to Rebekah and her son Jacob, was able to help David fulfill God's promise in the life of her son without stepping out of her position or resorting to deceit. She didn't take Solomon's future out of God's hands and run with it; rather, she submitted her case to her husband, who was moved by God to acknowledge that she was right and to help make it happen.

Rebekah received a promise from God concerning her son Jacob, and she went about making it happen. She left her husband out of the mix, and through deception set a plan in place that ended up robbing her of the joy of seeing her son flourish. She got her way, but she never saw her son again.

Bathsheba, on the other hand, also had a promise from David regarding Solomon's future. Instead of plotting her own course, she took the promise back to the one who had given it. She empowered her husband to make sure what he'd spoken would happen. She got the joy of seeing her son ascend to the throne, and she gained the privilege of sitting at his right hand.[4]

The principle here is so powerful. If God is truly the originator of the visions we have for our children, He is well able to bring these things to pass without any work of our flesh being involved. It is enough for us to speak into the lives of our children the words God places on our hearts. He waters the seeds we've planted and brings forth fruit that lasts. There's no need for manipulation or deception. God is faithful to back His promises with actions that manifest exactly what He said. Works of the flesh have results that are temporary at best and often disastrous. But when we submit our children and our concerns to God in prayer, in His perfect timing He always brings His will to pass in ways that are beautiful and lasting.

As mothers cover their children in prayer and speak words of wisdom and vision into their spirits, their fruit will come to bear in ways that make God smile and encourage your man to call you blessed.

Matters of the Heart

1. In what ways are you preparing the children in your life for the future?

2. How can you gather the wisdom needed to deposit soundness into the hearts of your children?

3. Why is it important to take time to speak with young people and give them a vision for the future?

The Passion of Purity

My dear,

Lest you get deceived by love as the world displays it, let me tell you what will help you capture the heart of the king in your life. There are no shades in true love. Love is pure. This love is what gains the trust and love of men. How do I know? It captured me and made me center my love on my Shulammite woman.[1]

I saw her from afar. She looked like a poem moving among the rows in her brothers' vineyard. She was raw beauty with no pretense. Natural and real and unaware of her loveliness. Oblivious to her effect. She moved soundlessly about her tasks focused only on the work of her hands being fruitful. Others celebrated her beauty while she took no note of it, even denying it. She was far from self-conscious, but it was clear she didn't like to call attention to herself. In fact, she was ashamed of her appearance and said that while she'd been busy tending her brothers' vineyard, her own she had not kept up.[2] This left me speechless. She was the most beautiful woman I'd ever seen. A rose among thorns.

The moment I saw her I desired her. I surrounded her with my chariots and invited her to come away with me. She acquiesced. I praised her beauty, and she praised me, saying she wished I were her brother so she could kiss me in public.[3]

This beautiful woman was so demure. A lady in every sense of the word. Though she was ardent and free in her praise of me, she kept her virtue. She said we should not stir up love until it was time. Though we desired one another, she was careful not to step over the line. She kept her body pure even though she'd given me her heart. She respected passion and didn't play with its fire. This caught my attention. So many women had pursued me and vied for my attention. They were willing to do anything. Many compromised God's standards and were willing to give themselves without any promise in return. I was bored and lost interest quickly. After a while they all blended into a sameness that made it hard to distinguish individuals. Kings love to conquer, and those women made it too easy to have them. I wondered who else had been privy to their attention.

My Shulammite was a virgin. I found this alluring. She was a garden that had been locked, a fountain that had been sealed. Only I would be given the key and granted access. This intrigue created an urgency in me to claim her. I married her. Would I have married her if she'd compromised herself? Perhaps, but I would not have held her in the same high regard. Because she held what was precious until the right time, she remained precious to me. She was not an easy acquisition. Something was required of me in order to win her heart. I've found that I value most that which costs me something.

I was glad she had brothers and friends who held her accountable. They confronted her when they saw our romance budding. They asked her if she was a door or a wall, in essence wanting to know if she was keeping herself pure. They offered to put boundaries in place to preserve her purity. She was able to proclaim that she was indeed a wall, that she had kept herself for me and knew that she would satisfy me when we were married.

You should have seen our wedding! She was flawless. A rare jewel shining in the midst of common stones. When she gave her love to me it was without inhibition. I had acquired something priceless! No one else had access to her. She was mine and mine alone. She outshone every woman I'd ever seen.

I had a thousand vineyards, but she had only one, which she willingly gave to me. She withheld nothing—but not before it was time. She knew the fine balance between sensuality and purity. She was sexy without being aware of it. Even her denial was provocative and made me desire her even more.

This is the secret that most women today don't seem to understand. Things that are too readily available become cheap and lose their value. But the things we have to wait for, save for, fight for, those are the things that are of great value and remain that way. Women who care about purity will be treasured because they're rare and beautiful.

I encourage you to love yourself enough to demand this exclusive love from your man. Allow him to pursue you. Let him win your love and earn your trust. Then, and only then, will you be able to rest in confidence that you have his heart.

Still in love,

Solomon

Man to Woman

Every man needs to feel he's received a valuable prize. A prize no one else has access to. A woman needs to know she's really desired by the man in her life. She can be sure of this if he pursues her with enthusiasm. If a woman manages to get a man that *she* pursued, she'll live with the insecurity of wondering if the man truly loves her because he wasn't the initiator.

While purity isn't a popular topic in today's world, a man's fantasy is still to marry a virgin. Though few men admit it, they wonder how many others have had access to the woman he's pursuing if she's compliant with intimacy before marriage. He wonders if she'll maintain her chastity after marriage. If he travels, or gets sick, or another situation interrupts their sex life for a time, will she remain faithful to him? Self-control before marriage indicates great self-control after marriage. These thoughts run through a man's mind over and over even if he never acknowledges them openly.

Though a man will test the boundaries of intimacy with a woman, he is ultimately pleased when she doesn't give in. This refusal to compromise raises his trust level. In his mind, if he can't have you even though you say you love him, you won't give yourself to any other man either.

Yes, we can call it male ego if we want. The cold, hard fact of the matter is that men judge women based on how we behave when we're with them. We set the course for how they regard and treat us by the behaviors we exhibit and the boundaries we set and exercise. At the end of the day, every man wants to feel he's conquered his foes and won his damsel's admiration and love. The harder he has to fight for the prize, the more precious it becomes and the more revered it will be.

The Truth of the Matter

If we want to be treated like royalty, we must conduct ourselves like queens. We must understand that we teach men how to treat us based on what we allow. As much as we complain today about the risqué images and lyrics flaunted in music, movies, television, and other media, we must take responsibility for those images. They've been created not only based on the fantasies of men but also on our behaviors and responses to them. Sometimes it's not so much what we do as what we tolerate that does the most damage. When we support genres and fashions that devalue women and accept them as just popular trends, we further feed into those images being promoted.

Yes, as women grow more desperate due to a perceived dwindling numbers of available men, some may lower their values to lure men to their doors. So, my dear, if you're throwing your body at men, how will you stand out from the masses as someone special with a rare gift to offer? I'm talking about avoiding a Costco/Sam's Club mentality. The more abundant the supply, the cheaper it gets.

God created women, and He holds them in high esteem. Unfortunately, many have lowered the bar on their standards, and their behavior affects all of us. God's Word sets specific guidelines about our bodies and sexuality that, if observed and followed, secure our hearts and emotional well-being. The enemy of our souls is out to destroy us. He knows wounded women wound men and influence them to live beneath the standard God has called them to. This affects the children too, and soon we'll have godless generations. Nothing is done in a vacuum, and nothing affects just one person. Actions have ripple effects that touch countless others.

Purity may seem a trite and outdated issue today, but it's foundational in the formation of relationships, marriage, family, and society. I believe the rise in the devaluation of women is in direct proportion to the rise in women compromising themselves with men. There is no longer a demand for respect because women aren't respecting themselves. Desperate, they are settling for less than the best, and it's costing them more than they bargained for.

When we return to God's way of doing things...When we learn the value of our bodies...When we guard our affections and love appropriately...When we wait for the right time to give ourselves...That's when we'll achieve more fruitful and fulfilling relationships. The trust that is established this way allows greater confidence in relationships, which helps set the stage for a healthy love relationship that will last and endure every test.

Matters of the Heart

1. Have you compromised in the area of purity? What were the results?

2. Do you have any fears that contribute to the temptation to compromise?

3. What steps will you take to practice purity from this point forward?

The Greatest Beauty Secret

My dear,

If you're wondering how you can be set apart from other women, I have some experience in this area. Because of my position as overseer of the king's harem, I've seen many women come and go.[1] Beautiful and diverse, they were all unique. But in some there was a special quality...an intangible difference that is hard to vocalize.

In the palace, the wives, concubines, and others lived together in one area but in their own apartments. They were always available in case the king called for them. Some were called regularly, and some were never called after their first encounter. Though some wives were acquired for political reasons, others had caught the king's fancy for a time. Some fascinations lasted longer than others, and as I observed I came to know why.

King Ahasuerus (aka King Xerxes) was a powerful man with a big appetite for life. He didn't become powerful by being passive. No, he was a conqueror and appreciated what he conquered. His wife Vashti had been his favorite for a long time. She was breathtakingly beautiful and a bit of a spitfire. She wasn't placid by any means. She was a woman with her own mind, which was a double-edged sword. The same thing that fascinated him about her became the very thing that displeased him.

After a very successful campaign conquering new territories, the king threw a celebration that spanned six months. Queen Vashti held a separate party for the women in another section of the palace. On the seventh day of the feasting, the king sent a request for Queen Vashti to come to court. He wanted to show her off because she was supremely beautiful. He requested that she wear her crown.

Perhaps Queen Vashti was standing on principle or just wasn't amused by the king's desire to put her on display, but she refused to come. Refused to come to the king! Can you believe it? She embarrassed the king in front of all his guests. This disgrace reflected poorly on the reigning monarch. The insult couldn't be ignored.

The king burned with rage and turned to his trusted officials for a recommendation of punishment. They said she should be banned from the king's presence forever because they were afraid other women, namely their own wives, would follow her example.[2] The king agreed.

Later, after his anger dissipated, the king regretted his decision. His advisors decided it was time for him to find a new bride. A search was launched throughout the provinces for a new queen. Oh, you should have seen all the young women! They came from near and far. Any form of beauty you ever wanted to see was present. Those in the court marveled, commenting that if they were king, they would have great difficulty deciding on one.

I agreed until I saw her...Esther, that is. There was something special about her. She was beautiful, but I can't say there weren't others who were more beautiful. Nevertheless, she stood out from the rest. She didn't scurry for attention. She was regal in a quiet way.

I decided she was my pick. I would groom her for the king myself. I'd spent a lifetime serving him, so I knew what he liked.

I appreciated Esther's spirit. She submitted herself willingly to my instructions, and the results were soon apparent. While the other young women got caught up in the lifestyle of the palace, Esther remained humble. I took personal care regarding her diet and toilette. While the other contenders were eating fancy fare, I made sure Esther ate the right things to maintain and heighten her beauty. And there were the beauty treatments—the oils that were used to soften skin, eliminate unpleasant and foreign odors, and please the senses. King Ahasuerus wanted his women to smell like him.

At the end of the year of preparation, each young woman got her turn with the king. They were allowed to select what they wanted to wear and what they wanted to take in to him. Few heeded counsel. Here again, Esther was different. When it was her turn to go in, she did only what I told her to. When I was finished helping her prepare, I stood back to admire my handiwork. She was extraordinary. Everyone admired her as she went by on her way to the king's apartments. Quietly, graciously, regally, she moved. "Focus on him," I told her. "Do not sell yourself. Allow your virtue to do that for you."

She must have done what I said because the next morning she was announced as the new queen. The king was so delighted with her that he threw a feast in her honor. She was every bit the queen I knew she would be.

This came to bear when a rather serious matter arose. Haman, one of the king's friends, decided to carry out a personal vendetta against the Jews. What mayhem erupted the day the king issued the decree that all Jews in his kingdom be annihilated on a specific date. Esther was unaware of what was taking place until her cousin Mordecai brought it to her attention and pleaded that she go to the king on behalf of their people.

Queen Esther told him she hadn't been called for by the king, and the penalty of going before him unsummoned was death. Mordecai sent back a very sobering message, saying that perhaps she'd been placed in the palace for the very purpose of saving the Jewish people. I watched her consider his words, and then she shut herself in her apartment to fast and pray. She solicited the cooperation of her attendants in this.[3] When the fast and prayers were over, I was there, ready to help her dress for the king just as I had for the first time she went in to see him.

I planned her toilette and wardrobe carefully. When everything was in place, I sent her on her way. It reminded me of the fateful time she'd been chosen to be queen. She looked just as beautiful. But it was the light from within her that really sparkled. Grace covered her. She was radiant.

It was quite a fearsome move—to go to the king unbidden. I'd done my best to make her a welcome sight. The rest was up to her and her God. I'd read her note to Mordecai, where she'd written, "I will go to the king, even though it is against the law. And if I perish, I perish."[4] She took my breath away. And obviously the king's as well.

He welcomed her with open arms, offering her up to half of his kingdom. What king does that? Only a king who has been completely arrested and mesmerized by his queen. Once again, she put him first. She served him not one but two dinners before making her request known. And even then she waited until he implored her once again for what he could do for her after giving him so much pleasure.

Esther made it known that she was Jewish and submitted her request to save her people humbly and in deference to the king's authority and wisdom. That only if he felt it was the right thing to do should he honor her request. She said she didn't want to be a bother. How could a man resist such a plea?

The king rose to defend her and save her people. He ordered her enemy, Haman, annihilated and then gave the queen all of his possessions. The king honored Mordecai for his part in foiling the plot and because he was related to Esther.

Was there ever another queen like Esther? I think not. I'd seen a lot of women in my day in that palace, but never one like her. She had mastered the inner beauty of a woman, and it was far more beautiful than the external, which says a lot. I didn't know her God, but I suspected He had a lot to do with who Esther was. She held to her faith firmly but quietly, and it showed in her countenance and every encounter she had. Submission to God borne out of her simple and genuine faith was her greatest beauty secret. I pray it will be yours also.

Faithfully yours,

Hegai

Man to Woman

While most men are initially moved by what they see, how we make them feel inside is the attribute that binds them to us. Many a beautiful woman has ended up not being attractive to a man because her character and personality left much to be desired. Every man longs to see honor and respect in his woman's eyes. A woman has the ability to make a man feel on top of the world or at the bottom of the junk heap. Her approach, her words, her attention feed him the strength he needs to be the man he is supposed to be. Like a moth to the light, a man is drawn to a woman who is confident in who she is and knows her worth. The woman who wears her beauty quietly and without it getting in the way of her genuine care for him will win his heart.

Though we live in a highly permissive time in history, men still look for chastity and purity. They want the assurance that we will be theirs and theirs alone. Trust is of paramount importance. They need to be able to rest in our faithfulness to them. Men want to know that we have their backs and are there for them. They want to know we are genuinely interested in them and the issues on their hearts.

If we are self-serving, men will lose heart as well as interest. The pressure of having to conquer the world every day leaves men vulnerable. Inwardly they struggle with how to stay on top of their game and maintain their stature in the eyes of the women they love. When a man knows that he has his woman's trust and support, he will soar.

When women have needs, how men respond has everything to do with how women present their concerns. We can make our men feel like heroes or foes. When we *inspire* them to address our needs without being demanding, men will move heaven and earth to come to our aid.

Our greatest beauty secrets will never be found in the bathroom or cosmetic counter. Our greatest beauty secret is what we harbor in our spirit.

The Truth of the Matter

Kings will be kings, and every man desires to be the king of his own personal kingdom. In order to truly be his queen, we have to master a few things, such as developing a beautiful spirit to match or exceed our external attributes. And adding wisdom. Some scholars believe Vashti was legally correct in not appearing when the king called because there were laws concerning how and when women could appear in public. However, often it's *how* a person stands on principle that makes the difference. If it's not done wisely, the person may find herself standing alone. And that's what happened with the queen. Vashti seems to have had beauty but not much wisdom. She should have chosen a different way to handle the situation...a way that would not have embarrassed her husband and put him on the spot in front of his friends and subjects. The mistake a lot of women make is believing they can't be replaced. Nothing is further from the truth.

Esther shows us that we can win a war without engaging in a fight. With quiet dignity she got what she needed from her man without flexing a muscle. Sure, her beauty was a factor in winning his heart, but it was her gracious spirit that kept his heart. And her spirit was sustained by her willingness to stay yielded to God and step out on the wisdom He provided. Esther was able to subdue fear and desperation and masterfully execute a strategy to get what she desired from her husband. She was able to gracefully serve him despite her pressing need. She put him first, and he reciprocated. Her lack of manipulation helped him be willing to do anything she asked because he was confident in her love and heart toward him.

I admire Esther. Did you notice she didn't make a move until she heard from God? Then she followed His direction and ended up more blessed than she could have imagined.

In a world where we're tempted to "make things happen" and "do" everything, it would serve us well to get back to the basics of simply being women...beautiful women inside and out. God honors that, and so do men.

The Heart of the Matter

1. What attributes of yours do you place emphasis on? Why?

2. In what ways do you nurture your inner beauty? What does your personal and spiritual toilette consist of?

3. How do you approach the man in your life when you have a need? How can you adjust your approach for better results?

The Attraction of Redemption

My dear,

It takes a special type of woman to get a confirmed bachelor to break his solitary run and decide to get married. For those of you out there who are wondering how to close the marriage deal, I want to tell you how I became a man willing to pay the cost to have my woman in my life forever.

I first saw her from afar. She was totally unaware of me watching her. I could tell she hadn't come for what some of the other maidens had come for. Though they were there to glean, they were dressed as if hoping to meet someone of marrying potential. But this woman wasn't like the rest. She seemed to not have a thought about her appearance. No, she came dressed for the task at hand. Her hair was pulled back, sleeves rolled up, face free of cosmetics except for the kiss of the sun. Her eyes were downcast, intent on her mission of picking up grain left behind by the harvesters. Her posture was different from that of the others too. This made her stand out as even more beautiful. There was something real and natural about her that drew my attention. According to my workers, she was consistent.

Coming early to glean in my fields and leaving late because she was so intent on gathering as much grain as she could.

When I inquired after her, I discovered she'd gained quite a good reputation. She was a widow and also a foreigner. In fact, in some minds she was the worst kind of foreigner. She was a Moabite. Israelites weren't supposed to fraternize with them or even pray for them, according to the law. However, her character was so exemplary that everyone seemed willing to overlook this major fact. They also shared that she was taking care of her mother-in-law, Naomi. Ruth's persona seemed to win people over. No one had a negative thing to say. In fact, she was admired for her dedication to Naomi.

Something about her loyalty made me want to protect her. This woman was still young enough and beautiful enough to be self-indulgent, and yet she'd forsaken her own land, culture, and personal comfort to come here to take care of an aging relative who wasn't even of her own blood. This Ruth was a rare woman, and the import of who she was didn't escape me.

I instructed my workers to leave extra grain for her to glean and admonished them that no one should disturb or harm her.[1] Though I chose to see the woman she was, I feared others might not be as discerning. Because she was a Moabite, they might feel they could abuse her and no one would mind. I felt it my duty to make sure nothing unseemly befell her.

One day I invited her to join me for something to eat. She was so humble, so appreciative. I found this refreshing. She harbored no spirit of entitlement. I sensed no spirit of flirtation either...just a refreshing sense of wonder that I would be inclined to extend kindness to her. One season melted into another, and she consistently showed up to glean in my fields. I asked her not to venture into anyone else's because she wouldn't have the benefit of my protection, and she agreed.

There was no coyness about her, no sign of her being interested in my wealth or status. Her eyes and words were devoid of guile or hidden motive. She was genuinely polite and focused on her task.

One night I fell asleep after threshing grain. When I woke, I was surprised to find Ruth lying at my feet. She explained that she needed a redeemer. That I was the next of kin in her husband's family, and she hoped I would fulfill the law by taking her as my wife. I was deeply flattered that she would ask this of me. She could have chosen a younger man, and yet she came to me. I told her I was willing to redeem her, but there was someone in the familial line who was first in line as redeemer. I promised I would deal with the situation first thing on the morrow.[2] I instructed her to go back to sleep, but to wake and leave before morning light so no one would see her and speak ill of her. When she left, I gave her provisions for her household.

I felt extra energy in my step as I made my way to the city gate. The family redeemer who was next in line for Ruth's hand arrived shortly after I did. I knew I had to state my case in a strategic way to get what I wanted. I broached the topic by mentioning that the field of Ruth's father-in-law, Elimelech, was available to be redeemed. Of course he wanted the land. Then I reminded him that if he took the land, he must also take Ruth as his wife. He deferred, saying that marrying Ruth would endanger his estate. Right there in the sight of witnesses, I pledged to redeem the fields of Elimelech, Mahlon, and Chilion, and marry Ruth.

You can imagine the response when the rumor mill spread the news that I was marrying the Moabitess. "How could he marry such a woman?" many wondered. For me it was easy. My mother had also been a foreigner who made her own place in this society. Yes, I knew a little about being on the outside and looking in. Perhaps that was part of the attraction. Ruth reminded me of my mother.

My mother was Rahab, a former harlot who protected some Israel-ite spies in Jericho and was invited to join them. God redeemed her life, changed her, and made her a credit to our society.

My desire was to have this woman named Ruth in my life for-ever. And so I married her, and we never regretted a moment. When she gave birth to our son Obed, I'm sure I was the happiest man on the face of the earth. Ruth was worth the wait! She was all I'd ever prayed for and more.

Are you looking for a special man? Are you looking to capture his heart? Start with your own heart—a heart that looks beyond your-self. Let your works speak well of you. Glean everything you can from the life you have, and be yourself at all times. Men are drawn to women like this. They want to reach out and protect women with these qualities.

Truly yours,

Boaz

Man to Woman

In a world where cosmetics are glorified and women have per-fected the art of creating their own faces to present to the world, men still appreciate the natural beauty of women enhanced by their beautiful spirits. Men seek loyalty. Hearts that reach out to others in service. Women who give of themselves to those they love. Men also look for quiet and chaste women. A woman a man feels he can pro-tect, provide for, and lead. They look for honor and respect because their spirits need to feel appreciated. Their hearts reflect God's heart, which desires honor and respect in the form of obedience and appre-ciation in the form of worship.

A woman who is able to voice her needs to her man usually wins his support and attention. After all, he needs to feel needed. He is wired to fix things, whether it be a car or a life. He needs to feel necessary in his woman's life, knowing his life matters in her world. There is something appealing about the vulnerable side of a woman. He feels safe to reach out to her, to offer himself and his help as a solution to her challenges.

And yet there is also a necessary balance. There is a difference between having needs and doing the best you can to handle them while being open to help and being a gold digger. Many men fear being taken advantage of these days. They don't want to be viewed as objects or as banks. They want to be men who cover and take care of their women because they are men.

When a woman views a man as a source of income or a way to acquire things, she'll eventually lose him when he sees through her agenda. No one wants to feel used. A man lives to be his woman's hero not her victim. He wants a woman who will say, "Do not ask me to leave you. Your people will be my people, and your God will be my God." This vow of faithfulness encourages a man to willingly pay any price to be with you.

The Truth of the Matter

God created man and gave him the assignment of covering woman. When Adam failed at his assignment and Eve disobeyed and ate the fruit of the tree of the knowledge of good and evil, the curse of striving to be fruitful came into play. The mark of a man's identity is his ability to cover, protect, and provide for his woman. This affirms who he is. The drive inside him to be the man God created him to be is overwhelming; therefore, he'll be attracted to a woman who pulls on his heart from a place of need, whether it is emotional, spiritual, or financial. When he knows she is depending on him, he will rise to the occasion.

A woman needs to know that her reputation precedes her. Remember, you never know who is watching! In today's story, Ruth was gleaning away, her only focus being to take care of her mother-in-law and herself. While she was focused on meeting the needs of someone else, her own blessing from God was in the making. Boaz was paying attention and making provisions for her.

So many women today believe they don't need men, but the truth of the matter is women do need men and men need women. God has made us in such a way that we need one another to balance life in a healthy manner. When we embrace our weaknesses and needs, we open the door to allow someone to fill in the gaps. This *is not* a bad thing! In fact, it is the beauty of God's economy. He makes us a community that is held together by love and gracious care for one another. Perhaps it boils down to meekness and humility, which is strength under control.

Let's face it: Ruth was a strong woman. She weathered the death of a husband, a move to a hostile, foreign territory, and poverty. Yet she endured and did what she could to continue moving forward. It was at this place of taking care of business that she met Boaz. She didn't posture or present a façade to him. She was who she was. She didn't attempt to hide her need to work.

The Word tells us that God resists the proud but gives grace to the humble.[3] Ruth's story illustrates that beautifully. Was Ruth looking for a rich man to marry? No, she was not. She was doing what she had to without complaining in order to make ends meet. Her gracious acceptance of her circumstances and the resolve to make life work not just for herself but also for her mother-in-law, an old lady with no more hope, caught the attention of Boaz and won his heart.

Perhaps your focus needs to be on where God wants you to be and what He wants you to be doing regardless of your circumstances. In this humble posture, God will provide for you in surprising ways, including bringing you into the presence of a man who is looking for a woman with a heart like yours.

The Heart of the Matter

1. How do you handle your vulnerabilities?

2. Regarding your needs, how open are you with the man in your life? What is your greatest challenge in being open?

3. Where is your focus? How much do you pay attention to the needs of others?

A Man's Weakness

My dear,

I know a lot has been said about my untimely demise, and I feel it's high time I address it. Perhaps I wasn't the best example of what a man who was called by God should be, but I cannot deny that though I was a man of God, I was a man first. Was I fully surrendered? No, I wasn't—until it was far too late to understand the error of my folly. While I was forced to learn things the hard way, I don't feel that was God's preference. This is why I've chosen to share my story with you. What you do with the information will be up to you.

My own weakness caused me to be attracted to the wrong women, but there is a reason why I was that way. My parents preferred that I choose a woman from among our own people because they didn't want me to be unequally yoked with an unbeliever. But to be perfectly honest, the women among my own people bored me. They believed serving God meant being uptight and rigid. They seemed to be uncomfortable with themselves and not fun to be around.

The Philistine women were very sensual, uninhibited, and not bound by so many rules. They acted free. Don't get me wrong—I have nothing against godly purity. It just seemed that the balance between femininity and holiness among the women from my home area was out of sync. The fact that Philistine women were so comfortable with themselves made them highly attractive. They knew what to do to make a man feel like a man. They exercised their feminine wiles and made me feel like I was adored and the hottest man walking. It was hard to resist...so I didn't.

Now, am I saying a woman has to have loose morals to get a man? No, I'm not. As a matter of fact, I'm totally against such activities. Given a choice, no man really wants what another man has had. I'm just saying that being comfortable with who you are as a woman is attractive to a man. And this the Philistine women did very well. They caught my attention and distracted me from the call God had placed on my life. I was willing to violate His rules concerning my life to fraternize and even marry one of them.

It didn't work out well for me. The woman I married betrayed me, and it incensed me to no end. She revealed the answer to a special riddle I'd given my guests, and giving away that secret cost me greatly.[1] I fulfilled my part of the bet and then went to the house of my father to calm down. When I returned to my wife, I discovered her father had given her to one of my best friends! In retaliation, I tied 300 foxes together in pairs, added torches, and set them lose in the Philistine fields.[2]

Perhaps I should have learned that Philistine women couldn't be trusted, but I couldn't seem to get my fill of them no matter how many times they endangered my life.

When I met Delilah, I forgot all my experiences and failed to see the signs that would lead to my demise. She was so beautiful—breathtaking, in fact. A real woman. She knew how to dress and make my imagination travel. She was an impressive hostess, serving the best food and wine. She knew how to make a house a home, and she made me feel like a king. All the while, she stroked my ego. She was all about me. She had no inhibitions when it came to making me feel like the center of her world. She was always telling me how strong I was. She was fascinated with my strength and wanted to know my secret.

I should have known something was up. I'd been in similar situations with my first wife, and she'd used my honesty against me. At first I wouldn't tell Delilah my secret, but she seemed so wounded by my reticence that I finally threw all constraint to the wind. She said if I loved her, I would tell her the key to my strength. Initially I felt a bit wary. I told her different things, and each time she used them against me. Then she accused me of making her look like a fool. She kept at me so long that I felt compelled to prove my love. I finally told her the truth—that my strength lay in the fact that my hair had never been cut.

Maybe she loved me, maybe she didn't, but one thing is for sure: She loved money and herself more than me. She sold me out. Imagine my shock after I revealed the source of my strength to wake up and find my hair gone and soldiers surrounding me. The greater shock was discovering the Spirit of the Lord had departed from me, leaving me to wallow in my own weakness and the hands of the Philistines. The soldiers gouged out my eyes and threw me in jail.[3] I became a disgrace and a laughingstock. I failed God.

Yes, the wrong kind of woman can make a man forget God and lose everything. This I found out too late. The wrong woman can sap a man of his strength and leave him for dead. She can distract him from his purpose and destroy his destiny. This is what Delilah did to me, and it resulted in a tumultuous relationship that led to my death. Don't be this kind of woman if you want a strong, lasting relationship.

I like to imagine how her feminine tools could have made our relationship outstanding if she'd been a woman of integrity. A woman who loved God and loved me would have recognized the calling on my life and supported it. She would have encouraged me to stay on the right path and serve God and my nation. The quiet conversation of her life would have impacted and influenced me to focus on and line up my life with my calling. She would have helped me clarify my purpose and live out the full potential of my God-given destiny because her desire would be for God's will and purposes to prevail. The right kind of woman knows how to make these attributes attractive to a man so that his greatest desires are to serve God and be a blessing to his woman.

Why am I telling you all of this? Because I learned too late the difference between the right kind of woman and the wrong kind of woman. I learned too late the value of pursuing a godly woman. I encourage you to be an exceptional woman and explore how to make that attractive. Explore how a woman of God can be a woman men desire. A man fulfilling his destiny may depend on you.

Seeing more clearly,

Samson

Man to Woman

In present day, people question whether purity is out of fashion. The answer is no. Men still want to have what no one else has been able to get. A virgin is a mystery and fascination for a man. A man is proud to have this type of woman to claim.

However, a religious spirit will kill any attraction a man has for a woman. Should she come off as too rigid, condescending, and judgmental in her beliefs, he'll feel rejected or not up to par. A woman needs to master the fine balance between walking in purity and exuding feminine charm. She needs to allow her man his humanity without making him feel judged and criticized. He doesn't want to be in competition with her pastor or held to a level he feels he can't achieve.

This is where honor comes in. No matter what level of spirituality he is on, if a woman gives him the room to rise to the full stature of his faith and convictions free from the pressure of nagging or disapproval, he will thrive. Remember, a man lives for the approval and admiration of his woman. He will do anything to achieve those things. However, if she makes it a mandate that he live up to her goals rather than being an inspiration to him, she'll lose him.

Please remember that while holiness is beautiful, it is an *internal* attribute. A man still looks at women externally. He is first moved by what his eyes see. A woman must not only possess godliness, but she must also take care of herself and be outwardly attractive. She needs to have a feminine presence accentuated by nice skin, an alluring figure, a light in her eyes, a smile on her lips, an infectious laugh, and all the other things that are appealing to the eyes and spirit of a man.

Understand that "sexy" doesn't mean doing anything "over the top," so to speak. Instead, sexy is something that exudes from a confident woman. And not one who is scantily clad or trying hard to be provocative. Some of the sexiest women in the world reveal very little skin. A wise woman balances her spiritual and natural attributes in a way that neither compromises her walk with God nor repels the man she wants to attract.

The Truth of the Matter

Many women today are desperate. I believe the shortage of available men has launched women into aggressive action to secure their men at any cost. Revealing attire and blatant sensual behavior are the orders of the day. Back in biblical times, the women of Moab lured the men of Israel into idol worship. In the days of Solomon, his love of foreign women, whether politically motivated or not, eventually caused him to compromise his walk with God, which led to depression and, eventually, his demise. Solomon sadly concluded that all was vanity. Such a brilliant start he had, and yet at the end of his days he was jaded and disgruntled.

A woman has the power to make or break a man. Many misuse their power, but some don't use it at all. Those who misuse their attributes for gain justify their actions by pointing to their acquisition of a man (or men) and the material gifts he gives as evidence that their attitude works. Today our eyes are assaulted daily in the media by brazen behavior and even enhanced body features accentuated by skintight clothing that leaves nothing to the imagination. This is not the type of woman a man honors and respects. He will often use that type of woman for amusement or as a temporary trophy though.

The type of man a woman of quality is really looking for isn't amused or attracted by manipulative women. A man (*not* a boy) is looking for a woman to walk through life with him. Someone who will complement, support, and partner with him. He wants her to be attractive. He wants to desire her physically, but passion is not nor should it ever be the primary focus of a man selecting a woman for a forever partner. Chemistry wears off. Life isn't easy, so no man wants a beautiful house with no one at home, so to speak. He needs substance, godliness, and beauty in one package. Someone who will strengthen him for his journey.

Sometimes Christian women, perhaps out of fear of falling, can be so rigid and legalistic they aren't free to be the woman they need to be to attract a man. Femininity needs to be cultivated in these women or, at least, relocated to a more primary position. Women in the world are using everything they have outwardly, but women who know God have the ability to pack a one–two punch! They have what it takes outwardly *and* inwardly. The balance of these virtues wins the heart of a man. Your ability to build his strength and not deplete his virtue is powerful.

Realizing that you have feminine power and using it to a positive end is the key to fruitful success in a romantic relationship. Failing to contribute to the call on a man's life or thwarting his purpose is a tragedy no woman should ever be proud to be part of. Please permit me to interject this truth: The call on a man's life may or may not be ministry. Whatever his career, being a godly man within his circle is the call on his life. A woman's influence can affect a man's integrity. Every woman makes choices on how to use her charms. Popular culture shouldn't dictate her decisions. The fear of the Lord should guide her so, at the end of the day, the man in her life will arise and call her blessed because he is a better person for knowing her.

The Heart of the Matter

1. How secure are you in your femininity? What is the difference between being natural and being sensual?

2. How do you respond to a man's attention? How do you find the balance between maintaining purity and being responsive?

3. In what ways can you add to the strength of a man?

The Need for Agreement

My dear,

Let me get straight to the point. One of the worst things you can ever do is to find yourself walking through life with someone you aren't in agreement with. I'm sure my story will help you understand why I'm so adamant on this point. I'm not going to dress up the truth to make it look pretty. One of the most painful things you can ever experience is not having the correct support in times of trouble. Yes, a man is supposed to be strong, but he is supposed to be made even stronger by his wife. She can build him up or level him to the ground with one word. After devastating her man, that same woman might wonder why he can't get his act together. That's simply not fair or realistic. Let me give you a full picture of what I had to deal with. Then you'll get my point.

I am a man who tried to do all the right things. I loved and honored God to the full extent of my ability. I tried to anticipate the things that might befall me so I would be ahead of the game. This I didn't do just for me, but for my family as well. I covered all the bases. When I offered sacrifices to God, I also offered sacrifices for my children...just in case they'd sinned against God. I left nothing to chance. I figured boys will be boys and girls will be girls, so I should cover them in prayer. I didn't pretend my children were perfect. I raised them in the way they should walk before God and hoped they wouldn't depart from it.[1] However I also understood that young people feel the need to learn things on their own and experiment in life. Sometimes they don't make the best choices. As a parent I felt the need to do what I could to secure their future and, hopefully, curry favor with God for them. After they gathered for their feasts, I would always do a sacrifice for them just in case, in the midst of their merrymaking, they had cursed or sinned against God.

I've heard it said that "conversations in heaven get us in trouble here on earth." I wasn't privy to anything specific, but suffice it to say that trouble came my way in droves. First my oxen and donkeys were stolen and my herdsman killed. As this news was sinking in, another servant arrived to tell me my entire flock of sheep had been wiped out by fire from heaven. Then someone else arrived to tell me all my camels had been stolen and my servants killed. Shortly after that another arrived to tell me the house had collapsed on my children, and all seven sons and three daughters had been killed.[2]

Can you imagine? I was shattered. Yet I refused to curse or blame God. He had been more than generous to me. I concluded that "the LORD gave, and the LORD has taken away; blessed be the name of the LORD."[3] It is His prerogative and His right as the Creator to move according to His own judgments.

Perhaps I internalized my grief too deeply. I spoke no words, so my pain manifested itself physically. I developed the most awful and painful oozing sores all over my body. I had no recourse but to sit among the ashes of my life and scrape my wounds. I waited before

God and strained to hear from Him. But I heard nothing. I continued to wait.

The look in my wife's eyes devastated me. Her disappointment and anger at God was mingled with contempt for me. "Do you still hold fast to your integrity? Curse God and die!" she told me. She practically spit the words at me. I wanted to die, and yet I could not. The way she looked at me hurt me more than all that had transpired. I felt truly alone. Alone in my misery. Alone in my suffering. Alone. *Nothing can be worse than being abandoned by your wife*, I thought. It was even worse because she was still with me but emotionally absent. Where does a man turn to then?

My friends came. Three of them. They traveled from afar. When they saw me, they expressed their anguish over my condition. And then do you know what they did? They sat on the ground with me in silence for seven days. Silently empathizing with me in my pain. If only my wife would have done that! Instead, she withdrew from me, which exacerbated my suffering.

So many emotions swirled about me. My questions remained unanswered. The pain of losing my children and, it seemed, my wife as well. How would I survive from all that I had lost? Where was my wife to comfort me? To weep over me? To commiserate with me over our circumstances? I was very aware that she too had lost everything. Our children meant the world to her. Far more than the other things we'd lost. As a mother, she mourned on a whole other level, but now was not the time to pull away from me. Now was the time for us to hold one another even closer. My friends couldn't replace her comfort. I longed for her nearness, her understanding. But I didn't receive it. I was left to face my distress without her. Thank God for friends who stick closer than brothers.

Where I was once considered one of the wisest men in the region,

I was now at the people's mercy because I had no explanation for my condition or the things that had befallen me. Days passed as my friends tried to find rhyme or reason for the tragedies that had occurred. Nothing seemed to be the right answer.

Finally God spoke. He said that all our suppositions were wrong and reminded me that He was God and could do as He pleased.[4] He instructed me to pray for my friends. Then God restored my health, my fortunes, and even provided a new family. All I lost was restored.

My wife had been foolish at a critical time in my life. That could have led to my undoing if I'd listened to her. I understand that frustration is very real, especially when life is falling apart and the one person you've always counted on to hold it together is no longer in the position to do so. However, that is not the time to kill the wounded. I needed my wife to stand with me and help me get through it.

The Lord blessed my latter days even more than before. He doubled my flocks and herds and blessed me with new children. There were none like them in the land, they were so blessed. But did you notice my wife isn't mentioned in the rest of my story? There is a reason for that. What is there to say after her display of disrespect and contempt? I urge you not to let my story become yours. Make sure you are supportive during your man's failures as well as his successes. Do nothing to earn his disregard or God's. Do what you can to attract God's blessings. This will lead to a life well-lived because God is forever faithful.

Blessed and restored,

Job

Man to Woman

The worst thing a woman can do to her man is kick him when he's down. There should never be a case where the helper isn't helping. Since men take what their women say so much to heart, we must weigh our words carefully when our men are feeling down and out. This is when a man is most vulnerable to the wrong influences. He is more open to receiving counsel when life happens and the circumstances are beyond his control. He's looking for a voice of reason and a touch of encouragement. He needs to know that his present difficulty doesn't make him small in your eyes. Your encouragement will help him muster the strength to rise from the ashes. If you degrade him further than his circumstances already have, you'll lose him altogether. His pride as a man will be shattered; his ego irreparable. This is an assault against the core of his masculinity. To make him feel less than or not enough creates deep wounds from which he may never recover.

Though you may be disappointed that the man you've always relied on to be your rock seems to be more like a bump on a log in the situation, allow him some recovery time. Because men are naturally fixers, your man's first instinct is to go into his shell to figure out how he can alter his situation. It is vital for you not to criticize him at this juncture.

Proverbs talks about a foolish woman tearing down her house with her hands, but sometimes the most destructive work is done with the tongue.[5] A man would rather be on the corner of a roof than in a house with a nagging woman who continually gives him grief or adds to his trouble.[6] When a woman messes with a man's mind, she cripples him. When he fails to produce because of her debilitating conversation or his failure to figure out how to recover from his setback, he'll feel an overwhelming sense of failure. He needs his wife to address his situation with sensitivity, to be a support, and to help him navigate through the problem. With her encouragement and support, even the most defeated man can dare to hope again.

The Truth of the Matter

As I've mentioned, for the most part, men don't do life well on their own. Blame it on their mothers, who tend to excessively nurture them. So when you finally get a man in your life, he may still be a little boy inside. (Yes, some are more mature than others.) At any rate, every man fears not being king and lord over his space in the eyes of his woman.

As I said, and it bears repeating: Women can build up men or crush them with one word.

The Word of God takes the time to tell women to respect their husbands. Obviously in the heart of God this is extremely important. Husbands are admonished to love their wives.[7] I find it interesting that God didn't tell wives to love their husbands, simply to respect them and submit to their leadership. God knew what would make a relationship healthy and keep all parties functioning at their best.

Since women are counseled to respect their husbands, this suggests that the opposite could really have a negative effect on a relationship. Perhaps this is why Job's wife, after telling her husband to curse God and die, is never referred to again. We don't know if Job's next set of children were hers or not. Remember when Michal criticized King David for dancing out of his clothes in front of the Ark of the Covenant? Her lack of respect caused her to remain childless.[8]

On the flip side, we see women such as Esther, who respect their husbands. These women end up in quite a sweet place in the kingdom as well as in their husbands' hearts. Abigail had her own tale to tell of remaining respectful while being married to a fool. She ended up married to a king!

A little respect can go a long way, even when the person doesn't seem to deserve it. The bottom line is evident: When we stay in the right lane, God sweetens our journey no matter how rough the path. He restores our men when their lives are shattered.

Matters of the Heart

1. What is your usual response when the man in your life doesn't live up to your expectations?

2. In what ways can you empower the man in your life to be a better man?

3. What specifically do you believe your assignment is regarding the man in your life?

The Price of Love

My dear,

I don't even know how to begin to tell this story. Being a prophet is a hard life. About this I cannot lie. We are called to do things that no ordinary person could or would do. Our lives become examples of truths that God is trying to convey to mankind. Sometimes the illustrations He asks us to play out can be a bit unorthodox. Take me for example.

I was so shocked when God told me to marry an unbeliever. It was bad enough that she wasn't devout in the things of God, but it was even worse because she was a known prostitute.[1] Many a man has married a woman thinking he'll change her ways or vice versa. The end of the matter is always the same—pain. I learned this the hard way. God used me to show the nation of Israel how He felt about them, and in the process I learned about God's heart and my own.

God told me He wanted my marriage to be an example of His relationship with Israel. My heart bled for Him because my heart bled for myself. This woman I married shattered my heart. When

God began airing His heart about Israel, I was taken aback at the strength of His pain and anger, at the depths of His heart condition toward the Israelites. He sounded like a spurned lover seeking revenge. He threatened to strip her naked and leave her to die of thirst.[2] He said He would refuse to love her children. Because Israel was a shameless prostitute, He would block her in with thornbushes and make it impossible for her to find the lovers she ran after. He would shut down all of her options until she was forced to think she'd be better off with her husband.

God went on to lament about how He'd been the one who gave her everything she had, and it hurt Him that she'd given the gifts He gave her to Baal.[3] He said He would publicly humiliate her, shut down her celebrations, and punish her for her adulterous behavior.

Then God turned around and said He would win her back again! That He would take her to the wilderness and speak tenderly to her and give her back her vineyards. He said He would renew her hope and wipe the name of Baal from her lips. He would again be a husband to her and renew His covenant with her. He vowed to make her His wife forever and shower her with compassion and love. He swore His faithfulness to her. All this He said to the one who had been so unfaithful.

Though He could find no faithfulness, kindness, or knowledge of Himself in the land, He swore that though she would suffer the consequences of her actions, He would redeem her from all her sins.[4] Though He had torn her to pieces, He would bind her up. He longed for Israel to look for Him and to show Him love. This He desired more than sacrifices.[5]

I wondered at this love until I experienced it for myself. I married Gomer, and she wandered off after other lovers. I don't know if it was my personal pain or my public shame that hurt the most. She blatantly disregarded and disrespected me by flaunting her lovers for all to see. God told me to go and love my wife and buy her back even though she had committed adultery. This was to illustrate His love for Israel and the extremes He would go to in order to win her back. So I went and bought Gomer back for fifteen pieces of silver and five bushels of barley.[6] I took her home and kept her secure. I would not allow her to have sexual relations with anyone, including me.

Though I understood the illustration God wanted to make, it was hard to comprehend this kind of love—love that loves despite disappointment and betrayal. What kind of love can take this hurt as deeply as I hurt and still want the woman back? Ah, but this is true love—real love, deep love, unexplainable love. The type of love God has for us.

I wasn't intimate with Gomer right away, but I was glad she was home. I wanted the assurance that she was safe from harm. I was sure that if I could just get her away from temptation she would see the error of her ways. To what could she compare my lovingkindness? I decided to take on the same tactic as God. I would woo her back with goodness. This she couldn't deny. No one would treat her as well as I did.

I marveled at my capacity to take her back after such a flagrant act of...of betrayal. Yes that was the word: "betrayal." Now I understood God's disappointment with His people. He'd invested in them. He'd nurtured and cared for them. He'd fought for them. For them to turn to and choose someone else who had never done anything for them would be the ultimate insult.

A man who has poured his heart and soul into being good to his woman will never understand why she might want to wander. His world is destroyed if she chooses to leave him for someone who is "beneath" him. It is difficult for him to stand in the face of that, and yet it becomes the greatest test of his love for her. His woman's response to him reaching out will make or break him. A man in love is determined. He will move heaven and earth to get his woman back.

Much is said about the wayward man, but little is said about the wayward woman. In a sense, we all are wayward when it comes to how we treat God. Yes, you should never have to question your man's love for you. If he loves you, he will love you in spite of yourself. There will be nothing you can do to separate from his love. If you stray, he will pursue you to the ends of the world to win you back and pay whatever price he has to in order to bring you to himself. That is the proof of a true, godly man's love.

Passionately,

Hosea

Man to Woman

Times have changed. Women have become more forward in love relationships. But there is something in the DNA of a man that makes him the hunter. When he loves a woman, he will work to win her love. He will not be deterred in the chase. The woman he has to fight for becomes a greater prize. He longs to win her heart and gain her love, honor, and faithfulness.

The blow to a man's heart is real if his woman becomes unfaithful. Most men don't recover from betrayal. This strikes straight at the heart of who he is as a man. The fact that he "wasn't enough" is devastating. A man feels that he has invested all he has, and if it wasn't enough, he's overwhelmed. His woman's unfaithfulness is a rejection of who he is and all he has done for her. It takes God to give a man the heart to seek her out and win her back.

Don't let it escape you that much of what your man does is

geared toward winning and keeping the heart of his woman. His career, his exploits, his gifts, his acquisitions, and his achievements are spoils of war for you. He works hard to be a success for you. He invests in you by providing for you. So, at the end of the day, if he discovers someone else has caught your eye and won your heart, he gets the message that he's not enough for you. The one thing a man can't accept is this pronouncement against him.

Please realize that when you have a man's heart, you have him. Be mindful of the gift your man is to you and treasure him. A loving, loyal, godly man is a rare find these days.

The Truth of the Matter

God created man in His image and with His heart. He has invested into us by even giving up the One who was dearest to Him— His only Son, Jesus Christ—for our sakes. The story of Hosea is a classic love story because it reveals God's pain when we wander waywardly after other lovers. These lovers come in many forms, including achievements, acquisitions, men, food—you name it. Anything that takes first place in our hearts becomes a lover or idol that stirs up jealousy in the heart of God. It is our ultimate rejection of Him after all He's done for us. We are casting Him into second place.

The same holds true for men because they are mirrors of God's heart toward us. Unfortunately, sometimes we don't appreciate a good man until he is gone. The tension of unavailability or that which isn't necessarily good for us can wreak havoc on the choices we make until we find ourselves in situations that lead to great regret. Not all of us will be fortunate enough to find a man like Hosea, who can hear God forgive his woman of her trespasses and then wholeheartedly seek to win her back.

Most men, when rejected, lean more to what God first expressed in the story: telling a wayward woman that she's no longer his, and he won't claim her children. He says, in effect, "I will make life hard for you so that you will regret your decision to be unfaithful to me."

I often wonder what Gomer's response was when Hosea showed up to purchase her back from her pimp lover. Did she marvel at that kind of love? I would have.

Sometimes being unfaithful isn't so much an action as it is a heart condition. We long for something or someone else. When we feel unfulfilled, we're most vulnerable and susceptible to being unfaithful. We put the people who deserve our love, time, affection, and consideration on the back burner while we pursue other things. We must forever guard our hearts and remain in an attitude of gratitude toward God, as well as toward the man He's placed in our life.

Sometimes our choices need to be made in consideration of how they will affect others in our lives. Love is far too precious to take for granted or discard.

Matters of the Heart

1. What makes your heart susceptible to unfaithfulness?

2. In what ways can you nurture love when you feel it waning?

3. How responsive are you to attempts at reconciliation when there has been a breach in a relationship?

What Faith Can Birth

My dear,

I think women underestimate what they bring to their men's lives. Sometimes our focus seems to be a bit off in these modern times. Many women are looking to get married because of what they believe husbands will bring to their world. Whether it be romance, finance, or something else, that is only a small part of marriage. You need to be mindful that you also have something to contribute to your man's world. Something deep, profound, and fulfilling.

I was betrothed to Mary. I looked forward to being her husband. She was a beautiful young woman. Soft spoken and reverent. She loved God with all her heart. When she spoke about His Word and His promises, a light would come into her eyes that was transfixing.

I knew of the promises of the Messiah. I knew it was prophesied He would come through my family line, but in no way did I see myself being an active part of the plan.

One day Mary came to me to tell me she'd been visited by an angel![1] The being told her she was going to have a baby borne of the Holy Spirit. This child would be the Son of God. I'm sure you can imagine how unbelievable that sounded. How could such a thing happen? It seemed ludicrous. Yet I couldn't reconcile the Mary I knew with someone who would lie to me about such a thing. Mary was a woman completely submitted to God. She was pure in heart as well as body. A virgin with an open heart to Him. As I battled whether this was fact or fiction, I considered "putting her away" to keep her safe. Even if I believed her, others would not. She would be labeled an adulteress and could be stoned to death as punishment. I couldn't leave her to such a horrible fate.

Then an angel visited me and reassured me that, indeed, Mary would bear the Son of God, and I would be His earthly father.[2] At first I didn't know what to say. Me? Why would I be bestowed with such an honor? Why would God trust me to raise His Son? What an awesome responsibility...and what a privilege.

When Mary went off to spend time with her cousin Elizabeth, I pondered the magnitude of what she was bringing to my life. This wasn't just her destiny; it was mine too. This situation was not of my doing; it was God's doing. He had seen fit to entrust to me the task of raising His Son with Mary. When Mary returned from Elizabeth's, I looked at her with new eyes. I purposed in my heart to care for her, provide for her, and protect the awesome treasure she carried.

The events surrounding the birth of Jesus were nothing short of miraculous. From our harrowing trip to Bethlehem when Mary was due to give birth to Jesus' birth in a manger, from the shepherds who were directed by angels to come and see our child to the visitation by the magi, we were continually astounded.

And then an angel told me to take Mary and Jesus and flee to Egypt because King Herod was seeking to kill our child.[3] From Egypt we heard of the cruel slaughter of the Israelite boys two years old and younger. We wept and held Jesus close, imagining ourselves in that situation. Yes, Jesus was the Son of God, but He was still our tiny baby.

God was faithful to keep us in exile until it was safe, and then He told us to go back to Nazareth. I raised Jesus as my own, and it was clear He was a different kind of child. He seemed wise beyond His years, especially when Mary and I had other children. I watched Jesus and marveled that I was part of God's amazing plan.

I recall a trip to Jerusalem we took when Jesus was twelve. We were three days into the journey home before we realized He wasn't among us. Mary and I went all the way back to Jerusalem. We found Him in the temple astounding the teachers with His knowledge of God's Word. When Mary told Him of our alarm and anxiety at finding Him missing, He very simply asked us why it hadn't occurred to us that He would be found in His Father's house. That actually jolted me. In my heart He was so much my own son, but in that moment my perspective was rearranged. Jesus was the Son of God. This truth hit me all over again. Though He was my son, there was a part of Him that was divine. I was in the presence of greatness. Even at His young age I could sense it. That feeling grew as He grew. I watched Him with His brothers and sisters, and though He was one of them, He was also set apart.

Mary and I discussed this. We spoke of His relationship with God. It was special, and we marveled at our son's understanding. He spent time in communion with God, and the look in His eyes told us that God revealed things to Him during their time together. We dared not trespass on those times or intrude on His thoughts. We wondered at His future and what He would do when He got older.

I taught him the skills of being a carpenter, although I knew His calling went far beyond working with His hands. When He began to travel beyond Nazareth to outlying regions, Mary and I knew at some point we'd have to let Him go. His cousin John had begun preaching about the coming Messiah, and his message was spreading. We knew something was getting ready to happen…something of deep significance that would be a catalyst for change. We were right.

I marveled at Mary through all of this. Strong, thoughtful, in tune with her son and God. It was she who got Jesus to perform His first miracle. Though He initially resisted, He finally acquiesced to her directions and turned water into wine at a wedding we were at. Now I knew why God had chosen her to be His mother. She was special, different, set apart in her own right. She was built to endure all that would come to pass: His ministry, His crucifixion, His resurrection, and the role she would play after He returned to heaven. I wanted to be there for her as she would be there for Him. This is what Mary brought into my life.

She took the life of this everyday carpenter and elevated it to a level beyond what I thought possible. That is the power of a godly woman. To inject and encourage the purposes of God into a man's life and help him live up to his assignments. Being the father of God is not what I signed up for when I was betrothed to Mary, but that became part of the story of my life. I saw my life as being a carpenter, but God saw me helping to raise His Son.

God's plan is always greater than what we have imagined. I pray that you'll be the woman He knows you can be and that you'll be a conduit of bringing His purposes to pass. This is the power you need to be aware of. You are a purpose-bearer birthing destiny into the lives of the men you love. Embrace the call. Though you may have a separate calling of your own, most likely part of your fulfillment as a woman of God lies in this assignment too. Be mindful, however, that if you're married, your call will not conflict with your husband's. Your call will add to his. God's ultimate design in marriage is to make you a power couple for His glory.

Purposefully yours,

Joseph

Man to Woman

Fact: Men need women. God said it, and it is true. For most men to live up to their full potential, they need the right women in their lives. A woman who knows God and hears His voice is vital to a man falling in line with his purpose and claiming fulfillment of his destiny. If that woman doesn't see what God sees for her man, she can take him fully offtrack and down some garden path. But when a woman walks in her directive from on high, her man aligns with her. Together they complete their God-ordained assignment.

A man needs a woman who can believe for the impossible, see the invisible, and hear the intangible. Men are bottom-line people who instinctively walk within the realm of facts and figures—the hard truth. Women are more instinctual, sensing things in their spirits, hearing the unspoken cues. A man needs that to balance who he is and to give him the courage to step out in faith to accomplish the things God speaks to him. A man depends on his woman to hear from God and partner with him in bringing what he feels led to do to pass. Her steadfastness in spite of circumstances keeps him on course. She is his balancer. The period at the end of his sentence. This is where his heart rests—in her hands for safekeeping. She gives him permission to dream. A man is only as great as the woman he walks with. His potential is best realized as she partners with him to birth God's vision. This is the fact most women overlook but need to be most cognizant of.

Your man's life is in your hands; his future influenced by your insights.

The Truth of the Matter

Women are intentional conduits of destiny in the life of men. Whether she is a mother who locates the gifts in her child, the sister who breathes on the dreams of a brother, or a wife who encourages her husband to fulfill God's call for his life. Women were designed to be "help meets" for men.[4] Some assignments God gives to a man are difficult to fulfill without a woman by his side. This is why a man must be careful when he selects a mate. That person could make or break his destiny if she wasn't designed for his journey or has a different agenda that pulls him off course.

The people we align ourselves with have everything to do with where we end up in life. Joseph was in the lineage of Christ through marriage. Mary was the entryway into his prophetic destiny. I'm sure that never in a million years did Joseph think his life would go the way it went. He had simpler dreams based on the reality he'd been privy to all his life. To raise the Son of God was definitely not on his list of things to do. Yet he married a woman who altered the course of his life and set him in a great place of privilege. Because of her presence, the course of his life was drastically transformed. This is what a woman does best when she is in tune with God. She puts her man on course for his life so that he lives up to his fullest potential.

Mary enabled Joseph to fulfill his prophetic call, and she nurtured her son Jesus to also fulfill His call. She prompted Jesus to perform His first recorded miracle. She released Him to do what He'd been born to do. She didn't hold Him back. She followed Him to the cross and released Him back into the arms of God. She accepted the call from God to birth the Son of God. She sacrificed her own desires to fulfill God's plan to deliver a Savior to the world. Oh, the heartaches she must have endured, yet she knew it was necessary and acquiesced.

This life we live is not an easy one. It's filled with challenges, but there is a purpose for them all. God aligns people to equip them to walk out destiny together. Every woman should be aware of what she can bring to her man's world. It's more than love and passion. Above all, it's about God's purpose and what you birth together for His glory.

Matters of the Heart

1. In what ways do you encourage the men in your life to fulfill their God-ordained purposes?

2. What part do you see yourself playing in helping your man live out his destiny?

3. Are you a hindrance to your man at times? What can you do to change that?

The Price of Guilt

My dear,

Perhaps I am being a coward, but I was the victim of a woman's wiles. While others might say I was a victim of my own bad decisions, I insist it was only at the prompting of my wife that I made one of the biggest mistakes of my life. Yes, she was my weakness. From the moment I saw her I had to have her. There was one problem—she was married to my brother. I was also married. It was complicated, but passion won out against my better judgment. I divorced my wife, and Herodius divorced my brother. Then she and I got married. I was so happy! And though my decision to divorce my first wife created political havoc that resulted in a war that I eventually lost, I didn't care. I had my beloved. She moved in, bringing along her daughter and my niece, Salome. And we were doing fine…until John the Baptist showed up.

John the Baptist was an interesting character. He was the talk of the country. He lived out in the wilderness, and droves of people went out to hear him preach. They called him a prophet. He wore camel skin and ate locusts and honey. He seemed to always be fasting, and praying, and telling people they had to repent because the kingdom of heaven was at hand—whatever that meant. They went to listen and be baptized by him. The Pharisees went too, but John threatened them with hellfire. A character indeed!

That baptizer! He feared no one, including me. He condemned my marriage, saying it was not right for me to marry my brother's wife. He said it to my face![1] I was perplexed, and fascinated, and angered by him all at the same time. Something about his words and the passionate way he preached about the kingdom of God arrested me. Though I would not respond to his cries to repent, I wanted to hear more.

Herodias was livid and hated him. She would fly into a rage at the mention of his name. She wanted me to kill him, to silence him. But I could not. He hadn't done anything wrong. He wasn't a criminal. He was entitled to his opinion, and what he said would not change my actions. But what John said grated against her and fueled her to spill bile. She wanted him dead and gone.

To tell you the truth, I thought I would have more trouble on my hands if I had him put to death. The people were enamored with him and clamored to see him. I dared not do anything to stir them up even more for fear I would get involved in something bigger than someone merely spouting philosophies that were harmless. But my wife would not let it rest. It became a bone of contention in my home.

To quiet the storm, I had John the Baptist thrown into jail. I hoped in time the matter would blow over, and I would be able to release him with the caution to never speak of my marriage again. Herodias fell silent, and I thought finally the matter had been put to rest. But I should never have underestimated the power of a woman.

It happened on my birthday. I threw a great feast in Galilee with guests that included military leaders, nobles, and leaders of society.

Our spirits were high. Salome, my stepdaughter, came before me and danced. I was completely entranced and so were my guests. I wanted to reward her for such a magnificent display. I asked her what she wanted and said I would give her up to half my kingdom. I waited in anticipation of her request. *What would be the young woman's pleasure?* I thought. *Would it be jewels and gold? A palace of her own? Rich, luxurious fabrics from some exotic land?* Imagine my shock when, after conferring with her mother, she came back and asked for the head of John the Baptist.

My heart dropped. That was not the answer I was hoping for. Now that she'd publicly declared her desire, I was forced to honor her request or lose face in the eyes of my guests. I couldn't believe Herodias would put her own daughter up to such a bloody thing. I'm sure that's not what the girl wanted. What young girl would ask for that when she had the opportunity to have anything else? At any rate, the request had been made. I ordered the head of John the Baptist be served to her on a platter even as I fought against the dread in my heart.

After this incident, the reports started coming in of a man named Jesus doing miracles. I was racked with guilt and fear over the death of John the Baptist, and I just knew this was him come back to life. Herodias thought this was ridiculous, but I was convinced. As time went by, Jesus became even a bigger sensation than John. He healed the sick and raised the dead. His followers grew out of control.

The Pharisees were uncomfortable. They murmured that He was trouble. They plotted and planned to get rid of Him. Finally they got one of His main disciples to betray Him. The guards arrested Him and turned the tide of public opinion against Him by accusing Him of heresy and treason. They brought Him before me and urged me to condemn Him to death. I wanted no part of it. The specter of John the Baptist still hung over my head. I still lost sleep at night over that man. I refused and sent this Jesus fellow to Pilate. Let him deal with it. Perhaps it was a coward's way out, but I didn't care.

From the day I had John killed, my life was filled with trouble. It finally culminated with me being cast into exile. There I lived out my days with Herodias. My peace was gone, and nothing could get it back. That one bad call haunted me the rest of my days. Guilt is a terrible overlord. In hindsight, I realized that perhaps Herodias was convicted far more deeply than I was by the words of John. For her, his death gave her the silence she needed to be free. But her freedom was the beginning of my bondage. I should never have allowed the situation to progress so far. Maybe John was right. Was it too much to accept that I was wrong and deal with the truth of the matter? In the end, condemning someone who made me feel condemned brought a worse penalty than a lifetime of regret.

Why am I telling you my story? Because it is important for you to realize that bitterness can entrap you and those you love if you allow it to grow. The price is too great.

With regret,

Herod Antipas

Man to Woman

Quiet as it's kept, a man is no match for a woman when she decides she wants something—especially when she goes into attack mode. She will exert pressure that can make a man feel he is incompetent. If he doesn't agree and resists the course she wants to take, she can make his life miserable.

A man needs to feel he has a say in every important matter. He wants his woman to trust his judgment enough to know he will make the best decision for all involved. In most cases, he may not voice his fears, especially if he is in a powerful position. He wants to appear invulnerable, so he may not be willing to explain why he has made the decision he has.

He will resent being pushed to do something he's against. He'll resist even harder the more his woman insists. I encourage you to read the signs and know the reason behind your man's stubborn resistance. If you persist and get him to do what he doesn't want to do, there will be a price to pay.

Anytime we make a decision based on anger, fear, or pain, it is usually the wrong choice. While women are sensitive to minor details, a man can overlook them when considering the bottom line. He's moved to respond based on his end goal for the situation regardless of how he feels at the moment. He will stick to his decision unless his woman mounts unending pressure on him. In the end, he may abdicate rather than continue to fight, but it will demoralize him and affect his future decisions. Remember, his decisions will ultimately affect you, so choose your battles wisely.

The Truth of the Matter

When we women get on a roll, it's hard for us to let go of what we think we want. Whether it's passion or being driven by some inner compass that is focused on the end goal of our desires, we can be insistent beyond reason and miss valuable cues to respond differently. We need to be cognizant that God will use the men in our lives to balance our perspectives or adjust the timing of our dreams. Our men have been given keen insights into the bottom line of matters. They usually aren't moved by emotion but choose to evaluate the situation to see what the end results will be before making a move. If they don't find the outcome beneficial in the long run, they'll opt out.

When we keep pushing against our men's decisions, we are, in essence, telling them we neither trust nor respect their opinions. This is hard for men to bear. It will eventually negatively affect their decision-making process. They will refuse to make any decisions and allow us to make them all. This will erode respect and eventually love in the relationship. Women find it hard to love men we don't respect. We won't desire them intimately because we feel no sense of power from them.

And yes, women are attracted to men who exercise power even as we push against it. This is the struggle that began in the Garden. Just as Adam got in trouble for not covering Eve and yielding to her bad decision, a lot of men fall prey to that today. When we pressure men into making bad decisions, we also have to live with the consequences of their bad choices.

I've often thought of how the entire scenario must have played out. Herodias obviously was painfully convicted by John the Baptist's words and wanted to silence him and clear her mind of his voice. As long as he was alive, he was an unpleasant reminder of what she'd done. And then there was her daughter. I'm sure Salome resented her mother for making her use her "winning chip" to request a prophet's head. She could have had up to half of Herod's kingdom, and her mother made her waste her opportunity to grasp something of import. Herod also was impacted by Salome's choice and became paranoid. His only sign of recovery was refusing to have anything to do with the case of Jesus. He wanted no part of it because he knew how he'd been robbed of peace of mind regarding the death of John the Baptist. We will never know the depths of how that decision affected him. I'm sure he was haunted by it. Perhaps it was the root of his demise since he ended up exiled until he died.

We need to strive to never misuse our power or pull others into vendettas.

Consider Queen Esther, who empowered her man to defend her instead of manipulating him to deal with her people's enemy Haman.[2] Of course, it's important to note that God had her back and was in charge of her mission. When God is behind you, He will contend with those who contend against you. Woe to those who pick fights on their own. Things did not end well for Herod and Herodias. Their fight was born out of flesh and sin, not the Holy Spirit; therefore, it could only have one ending. Bitterness and manipulation kill everything they touch.

You should always examine your motives for why you want what you want and consider how others will be affected before you encourage others to join your campaign.

Matters of the Heart

1. When you're confronted with a truth you don't like, what is your first response?

2. In what ways do you encourage others to take on your causes?

3. How open are you to being corrected when you're angry, in pain, or offended? What do you need to keep in mind at times like those?

The Power of Spoken Words

My dear,

I learned the hard way the importance of a listening heart that rests on the promises of God. It's ironic that I was a priest of the Most High, and yet I still struggled with faith. Who knows—perhaps it was the regimen of habit that made me settle into apathy when it came to God. Or maybe I was a bit jaded from watching others struggle before Him without finding answers to their questions.

I had served God faithfully for years on end, but still my wife was barren. We were both from the Levite lineage in service to God. My profession was looked on as fruitful, but our personal lives looked fruitless. This was a mystery that I chose not to complain about or question, but the unanswered desire lingered in the air. I purposed to serve God with all my heart despite not being blessed with children. And then one day life changed forever.

I stood in the temple before the Lord, lifting my heart, along with the incense I burned, in worship before the Lord. An angel appeared on the right side of the altar! He told me that my wife,

Elizabeth, would bear a son! Well, you can imagine my consterna-
tion as I considered the fact that we were well along in years. The
angel said God had heard my prayers. Do you know how long I'd
prayed for a child? Years. I'd given up and decided it wouldn't happen after we reached a certain age. Not only would I have a child,
the angel said, but this one would be filled with the Spirit of God
and lead many in Israel to repentance.[1] He would be the forerun-
ner of another, greater One to come. He would walk in the spirit
and power of Elijah.

My head was swimming. I struggled to take in and comprehend what the angel said. It seemed so incredible after such a long
time. And not only would my wife and I have a son, but he would
become a prophet specially called and anointed by God. It was hard
to believe. Even for a devout priest like me. How could this prophecy be true?

This question betrayed my lack of faith, but it didn't deter the
angel from the news he delivered. He confirmed that it was indeed
true. He went on to say the child's name would be John. *John!* There
was no John in my family lineage. Our custom was to hand down
the name of the patriarch, so this didn't make sense. It was as if the
angel read my mind. He told me I would be mute and remain so
until the child was born because of my disbelief.[2]

When I came from the temple, I couldn't speak. The people supposed that I'd seen a vision, but this hadn't been a vision. It was real.
I couldn't relate this to them though. I returned home after completing my time of ministering before the Lord. And just as the angel
said, Elizabeth conceived! We were elated! She didn't breathe a word
to anyone. We didn't want one negative thing about our situation
spoken aloud. My wife kept to our home for the first five months.

In the sixth month, we were visited by one of Elizabeth's cousins.
When Mary came, the baby inside Elizabeth leaped in her womb.

Elizabeth prophesied about the baby Mary carried. I was privileged to be standing in the presence of two miracles!

Again I considered how long Elizabeth and I had walked righteously before God. I wondered when we'd settled into going through the motions of belief instead of passionately pursuing Him and really believing in Him for the impossible. Where had our indifference come from? Perhaps from years of unrealized dreams. Or from subconsciously placing limitations on God as well as ourselves. God moved in spite of us! And here before me was the proof of His power and His faithfulness.

Finally the day came when Elizabeth delivered a boy, just as the angel had said. Oh what joy and jubilation! Relatives and friends came from near and far to celebrate with us. On the eighth day, when it was time for the naming and circumcision, everyone assumed the baby would be named Zacharias. When Elizabeth said the child would be named John, they were taken aback and protested that there was no John in the family line, so that name just wouldn't do. So they came to me to ask what the child should be named. I asked for a writing tablet and wrote, "His name is John." They were all shocked. Even more so because immediately my tongue was loosed and I could speak again! I stood and began praising God.

Many wondered at the significance of these happenings. What manner of child would John be? The Spirit of the Lord came upon me, and I began to prophesy. God gave me His words to declare over my son. He would be a prophet. God had visited His people and would redeem them from the hand of the enemy. My son would turn hearts back to the Father and instill righteousness in His people. Truly it was a time to rejoice! God was very real—more real than we'd ever realized. His people were still on His mind. He had not forsaken us. He longed for us to be in right relationship with Him. And my son, John, would be part of His plan to redeem us. I watched with joy as my son grew and fulfilled the words that had been spoken about him.

In all these things, Elizabeth had never expressed doubt. When I wrote down the vision I had and submitted it to her, she'd nodded knowingly and never questioned its validity. Perhaps she already knew and had harbored it in her heart while she waited for God to give me the revelation. Not only was she prophetic, but she was also wise. Her quiet faith ignited mine and gave me the boldness to go against the norm and name my son John as the angel Gabriel had instructed so the prophecy would be fulfilled.

Our words have creative power! It's best not to delay or undo God's work with our disbelief or words. When struggling to receive something by faith, sometimes it's best to quietly wait on God to manifest His promises. My wife taught me that sometimes silence is more powerful than speaking, especially when my words aren't fueled by faith.

Elizabeth birthed the promise and I learned that prophecy is not a questionable prediction but a true promise from God. My dear, the best thing you can ever do for your man is hold the things God has promised him close to your heart and help breathe life into them. He'll love you for it.

Blessed beyond what I believed,

Zacharias

Man to Woman

Every man needs a woman in his life who can keep the faith when he falters. (Okay, there are some exceptions, but they're rare.) I believe men are wired to be fruitful, have dominion, and subdue evil, so the inclination to make things happen is deeply embedded in their spirits and psyches. When they can't "make things happen," they take it very personally.

There is always the tension of what we can do and what God will do in and through us. We strive and strain to the point of exhaustion, and when things don't happen we search for avenues of blame. This can lead to settling into a new reality that perhaps what we'd hoped for wasn't realistic. When God interrupts our reality, it may be difficult to grasp His promises. We're reluctant to embrace what has been denied up to that point.

The woman in a man's life has the capacity to stir his faith and partner with him to believe God's purpose will come about. When a woman stands with her man and champions his faith, when she willingly stands in the gap and helps keep him engaged when he can't see the invisible, they can birth something powerful together that reignites the fire in his heart. This reignited fire will take your man to a new level in his walk with God. This is the man who has new visions for the future now that he's scaled the wall of unbelief.

Elizabeth's quiet faith spoke volumes and helped Zacharias silence his doubts. Unlike Job's wife who encouraged her husband to curse God and die when the chips were down, Elizabeth chose to hold her peace and see what God would ultimately do. I encourage you to aspire to Elizabeth's view and attitude. Trust in the Lord and believe His promises.

The Truth of the Matter

It's easy to stop believing for something when we've attached an expiration date to our faith. Since out of the abundance of the heart the mouth speaks, we can spout words of unbelief that affect our actions and the atmosphere around us, making it unconducive for miracles.[3] The power to believe for the impossible is fueled by the Holy Spirit. We need to make ourselves available to Him to perform God's will through us.

What ignites faith is the understanding of the purpose attached to God's promise. If the desire is personal, the ability to believe will be difficult because it's not attached to anything foundational. When God gives a promise, our desire is attached to a purpose that has an impact in His kingdom. When it comes to birthing dreams, we may not always understand the impact of them, but we can trust that God has a higher purpose than our personal desire. We may not have the insight that Elizabeth received, but we can still fully trust in God and His motives. Elizabeth understood fully that her son would be a powerful prophet who would do tremendous things for God and be instrumental in pricking the conscience of the nation of Israel. When Zacharias finally got beyond his own unbelief and saw the power of God at work, he too was able to prophesy and repeat those things spoken in the throne room in heaven concerning his son.

Recently I had the opportunity to witness this sort of miracle. One of my dearest friends disappeared from view. I tracked her down because she was being evasive when I suggested a visit. Finally, after several months, I insisted on seeing her. I showed up at her door. There she was hugely pregnant. Now, you have to understand that my friend was fifty-one years of age. She'd prayed for children for years throughout her marriage and suffered many challenges in being able to bear a child. Today she is the mother of twins! Two beautiful and perfectly healthy little girls. A total miracle! No artificial means used. Simply two surprises from heaven.

She later showed me her prayer journal and a page where she'd written her confessions that she declared every day during her prayer time. The pages were yellowed and frayed because she'd been praying so long. One of the affirmations read: "I am the mother of twins." She said there were times she wondered if it would ever happen or if she should just give up and stop praying, but she never voiced her doubts. She continued to hope in her heart. Finally her trust that God could do anything manifested in her heart's desire coming to life. Her husband stood in faith with her, and together they birthed a miracle. No...*two* miracles!

When we get to the place where we've exhausted our faith either for ourselves or the people in our lives, there is power in silence. Let us not conclude the matter aloud simply because we see no visible evidence of God at work. Instead, we can harbor faith in our hearts that God knows best and will work out the optimum for our lives. This leaves the door open for Him to do what He does best: birth miracles.

The Heart of the Matter

1. What is your first inclination when you experience disappointment?

2. When dreams or desires take longer to come true than you thought they should, does it affect your attitude toward God? What is the motivation behind the things you're believing for?

3. How capable are you of standing in the gap and undergirding the faith of others? What is the difference between standing for others and believing for yourself?

How to Change a Man

My dear,

If you've ever wanted to know what it takes to change a man, I'll tell you. It may not be the explanation you're looking for, but this is what I've learned regarding the influence of women. I walked with Jesus for three years, and I saw things that would take many books to tell. Some occurrences stand out more than others. There were so many different encounters with people and many miracles performed. If I hadn't been there, I'm not sure I would have believed the reports. But I saw it all for myself.

I never knew what to expect when walking with Jesus. On one particular day, He decided we should go through Samaria. I was surprised because few chose that travel route. It was fraught with danger, including armed robbers. No, this was not the route of choice. The other disciples and I looked at each other. You know, that "here He goes again" look. Yet, if that was the route He wanted to take, we would follow.

At one point on our journey, Jesus stopped to rest by a well. The other disciples and I decided to go in search of food. He stayed behind, but I wasn't sure why. When we returned, we were surprised to find him in deep conversation with a Samaritan woman. I studied her as we walked up and wondered at the nature of their talk. There was something about her...the tilt of her head...the light in her eyes. She didn't allow her focus to leave Him. It wasn't until we drew closer that she broke her gaze and acknowledged our presence.

The air was thick with our unasked questions when we arrived. Neither Jesus nor the woman seemed to find the situation awkward. Finally the woman took her leave. Jesus watched her head back to the village.

We looked at each other and wondered if we should ask what had happened. She was an attractive woman. She didn't act like a married woman, yet she carried herself with self-assurance. We noticed she'd left her water jar. We called after her, but she didn't turn around. She seemed to be in haste. We were quite bemused by this. After all, she'd left what she came for! We gazed at the jar sitting there. What had transpired that would make her forget it? We looked at Jesus, but He didn't offer an explanation.

We ate in silence and then wondered why we weren't moving on. Jesus seemed to be waiting for something. Night would be falling soon, and then our travel would become dangerous. Were we going to stay here longer? Jesus seemed quite happy to sit and bask in the afternoon sunshine.

Then we saw her. The same woman. But now she was followed by men...lots of them from the village. She beckoned them on, and they came forward with much curiosity on their faces. When she got closer, she motioned toward Jesus and said this was the man who had told her everything she'd ever done.[1] Could He be the Christ?

They all looked to Jesus, studying Him as they waited for a response. These men of Samaria didn't worship as we Jews worshipped. They had their own approach to God. They said everyone could worship in different places than we believed, so we left them alone. Now they stood inquiring about what we believed. And they asked on whose authority did we stand to believe something so contrary. They seemed to truly want to know the truth.

Then Jesus spoke. He shared the heart of the Father with them. All the while, the woman sat in rapt attention. The look on her face changed from one with no hope to one filled with hope. She transformed in front of us. So did many of those who had followed her!

We remained there for two days, sharing the good news of the kingdom of God and what God required of us. Jesus told them God was searching for worshippers who would worship Him from their hearts. Gender didn't matter. Race didn't matter. Where they worshipped didn't matter. All were welcome to come to God. Finally they were satisfied with all they'd heard. They turned to the woman and told her that now they believed, and not because of what she'd told them but because they had come, seen, and heard Jesus for themselves. [2]

At last Jesus was ready to move on. The people dispersed back to their homes, the transformed undoubtedly transforming others. An entire village had come to see Jesus because of one woman. She hadn't pushed her beliefs on them. She'd simply asked a question, "Could the man I met be the Christ?" Her countenance had certainly convinced them that she'd been transformed. Something about her was different, and that difference ignited their desire to know what could make that happen. Whatever it was, it was real and they wanted to experience it themselves.

This woman many had shunned and gossiped about became the catalyst to a village for seeking the truth. This woman stands out in my mind from most of the women we met. Those who traveled with us and invited us into their homes were amazing, but this woman ignited others *en masse* to change. This was the work of the gospel in a different way. Her words and changed look revealed her story and compelled others to reach out to Jesus.

As I mentioned, there are so many stories I could tell, but this one I enjoy because it shows the power of one person impacting her community. She didn't have a strategy. She just shared the earnestness of transformation. Sometimes *we* must be the change we're looking for in others. I must confess that I'd drawn my conclusions about her, but my opinion was changed by her earnestness. God's Word says we should share Christ as often as we can. I believe we should use words only when necessary. Take note that many battles can be won when we allow God to perfect change in us, which may cause others around us to hunger and thirst for more of Him based on our transformation rather than on the things we say. Many changes can occur when the change is evident in us.

A changed man,

John

Man to Woman

I've heard that women have thousands of words more in their vocabulary than men. That doesn't mean they need to use them all. The average man uses fewer words than the average woman; therefore, it stands to reason that his capacity to take in a barrage of information should be considered. Ask a man and a woman to tell you how their day went, and the length of conversation will be considerable—with the majority being offered by the woman. Most wise women know that when talking with a man it's best to get straight to the point. To dwell on long and winding tales is to lose him. Watch the glaze come over his eyes as he tunes out when he feels the story gets too long and laborious. Men prefer broad strokes and the bottom line. They are not into the fine details if they don't point to the end result. If a man has to follow and figure out what you're talking about, most of the time you can kiss effective communication goodbye.

If you want a man to change his mind about something, hammering away at your point will get you nowhere, especially when it comes to things of God. The Word tells us that an unbelieving husband may be won over by the quiet conversation of his wife.[3] This isn't talking about talking. It's referring to the *visible* changes in a woman that can trigger a transformation in a man. Obvious change can be more convicting to his heart than vocal conversation.

The conversion experience is borne out of illustration and understanding. As a woman allows God to shine through her, her man, and even coworkers, and friends, and relatives are more willing to open their hearts to receive from her example. For a man to receive what you're giving, the desire to change or the desire to please you has to be birthed in him. This will come about through the way you carry yourself. The way you treat him. Your willingness to address things you ignored before. The change in your countenance. How you serve or love him. Your sense of peace, joy, and fulfillment. When your man sees these things operating differently, it will move him to examine himself. The finger can no longer be pointed at you for distraction because three more fingers will be pointing back at him.

Remember, conviction must come before change. And no one will change until he or she feels the need to.

The Truth of the Matter

Sometimes the power of example is far more provocative than the spoken word can ever be. There is a thin line between "a time to speak" and "a time to put your walk where your talk is." People are looking for proof; therefore, let the proof be in what they witness in you.

I recall when I first came to Christ. My conversion was so dramatic that it drove my mother to inquire to those around her what had come over me. In the process of investigating the radical changes that had taken place, she too accepted Jesus and was born again. As a matter of fact, that happened to several of my friends and coworkers. When I tried witnessing to them and telling them about Jesus, they resisted or avoided me. Finally, the Lord told me to be silent and let my actions speak for Him. Time passed, and people noticed the way I'd changed. One by one they came to me seeking an explanation. They invited themselves to church with me to see what had gotten hold of me. One by one they gave their lives to Jesus. My personal change created changes around me.

Sometimes we're so busy looking at others and thinking about how they need to change that we overlook ourselves in the equation. Perhaps their actions are reactions to our actions. If we fail to look in the mirror and allow the Lord to do the work that needs to be done in us, we won't be very successful in sharing His love with others.

The Samaritan woman at the well was willing to deal with her personal truth, even though that truth was hard and difficult to swallow. She had to deal with breaking the cycle of disappointing relationships in her life, coming out of her shell, and confronting some things head-on. Everyone must do this! We don't want to miss opportunities to change for the better, get ourselves free from bondage, and help free others from their self-defeating actions. Our willingness to change makes the idea of change less scary to others. As you are, so will others be around you.

Matters of the Heart

1. When you're confronted with the truth about yourself, what is your typical first response?

2. What changes seem overwhelming just considering them?

3. How do you broach the topic of changes you'd like to see in the man in your life? In others? How receptive are they? Do you need to change your approach?

A Woman Who Dreams

My dear,

Let me tell you about the day a woman—my wife—saved my life. I suppose I need to give you the backstory in order for you to fully understand. I'd heard about Jesus, but I never thought I would meet Him face-to-face. His fame had spread, and He was some sort of superhero among His people, the Jews. Rumor had it that He had the power to heal the sick. That He drove out demons. That He brought the dead back to life. He was quite the sensation, and He made the Jewish Pharisees and other leaders very uncomfortable. The more His fame grew, the more incensed against Him they became. They felt they were losing their hold over the people. Jesus did and said things that flew in the face of their theology, and it diminished them in the eyes of many Jews.

So the Pharisees acted. They justified their actions by saying they were just thinking of what was best for the people, that they sought to keep the peace, that they feared Jesus would incite the people to rebel against Roman rule...so Caesar would get wind of their rebellion and crush them.

In light of our occupation of the area, the Pharisees had become powerful in their own right. They controlled the people by playing on their guilt and fear. They ruled with a tight, legalistic hand that put the people into even further bondage than our Roman rules. The Pharisees didn't like anyone who upset their system or usurped their authority. But the Pharisees did make it easier for me to control the Jewish population, and I appreciated that.

Anyway, enter Jesus with His disturbing questions and scandalous declarations that undermined the Jewish Sanhedrin's base of authority over the Jews and their temple in Jerusalem. At first the leaders sat back, hoping Jesus would be a one-hit wonder. That interest would eventually die down, and everything would get back to the way things were. Other popular prophets had come and gone, so why not Jesus? When John the Baptist had risen in popularity, he'd been beheaded by order of Herod Antipas, the monarch appointed by Rome. The people moved on...on to Jesus. And so even though He seemed a bit more spectacular than John, the Pharisees waited for His popularity to wane or something to happen to Him.

But Jesus defied their hopes. His popularity continued to rise until the people were in a frenzy to follow Him whenever they got wind that He was in a particular place. Apart from the miracles Jesus supposedly performed, He made claims that drove the Pharisees mad. They said that He claimed to be the Son of God. That He would rebuild the temple in three days if they tore it down. Ah, but the *pièce de résistance* was when he brought Lazarus back to life. I'd heard He'd raised others from the dead, but this time was different. All the other cases had been shortly after the person died. But in this case, Lazarus had been dead and in his tomb for four days! This was a miracle beyond understanding. The news spread like wildfire.

People came from near and far to see Jesus and Lazarus. This was the final straw for the Jewish leaders.

When a disciple who no longer liked Jesus' focus came forward, the Sanhedrin had what they needed. Judas was disgruntled that Jesus wasn't leading His people to revolt against Rome. Jesus wasn't cooperating. The follower felt Jesus had too much heaven on His mind. He believed Jesus needed to be stopped, so he made a pact with the Pharisees to help bring Him down. He sold Jesus out for thirty pieces of silver. After Judas revealed the place where "the prophet" could be taken, the Pharisees had Jesus arrested, bound, and put in jail.

The Pharisees dragged Him before me, but I sent Him to Herod because Jesus was a Galilean. But Herod wanted nothing to do with the death of yet another prophet, so he had Jesus sent back to me.[1]

I must say, the first time I'd been excited to see what this Jesus looked like up-close-and-personal. But when I saw Him, He wasn't what I expected at all. He was bigger in my mind than He actually was. He was a slight, ordinary-looking man who walked with humility.[2] Why would anyone see Him as a threat?

Yet...there was something about Him. Even now, after being beaten and subjected to various abuses at the hands of Herod and the soldiers, there was something almost regal about Him. His demeanor wasn't what I expected from a person in that situation. He didn't insist on defending Himself or His reputation. I questioned Him and found Him innocent of any charges Rome might levy against Him. I didn't see what the big deal was. Yet the Jewish chief and elders of the Sanhedrin were insistent that He be put to death. I figured it was fear and envy.

I was no angel. I had my own field day with the Jews. I was

responsible for the death of many in an effort to keep my status and position as the governor of these volatile parts. But I could find no fault with this man before me.

Seeing it was a holiday and traditionally the Israelites were entitled to choose one prisoner to be set free, I offered them a choice between a known murderer by the name of Barabbas and this Jesus, king of the Jews. Surely they wouldn't pick a thug. Jesus was harmless, and as far as I could tell had never hurt anyone. Imagine my shock when the crowd chose Barabbas! The Jewish crowd was fickle indeed. Were not these the same people who had wanted to crown Jesus king a short while ago? Unbelievable.

In the midst of deliberating, I received a note from my wife advising me to take no part in the death of this man. She'd been troubled by a dream. I'd learned not to take my wife's dreams lightly. It further confirmed my judgment regarding this strange, seemingly ordinary man who stood silently before me.

I questioned the crowd hoping to jar their consciences, but they grew even more fervent in their request. Because of my past record of upsetting the religious community and feeling some affinity with Caiaphas, the high priest of the Sanhedrin, I decided to wash my hands of the entire affair. Jesus' blood would not be on *my* hands. They could do what they liked, but it wouldn't come back to me. I felt a tremendous sense of relief. Thanks to my wife, I wouldn't be blamed for the man's death. My relief was confirmed when I heard that the disciple who had betrayed Jesus hung himself because of guilt and remorse.

I felt lighter when I went home to my wife. She had the capacity to dream and the discernment to warn me of dangers unforeseen. What a priceless gift! I had come to learn the distance between a bad decision and me was my wife. She inspired and encouraged me.

I encourage you to be sensitive to what goes on in your man's life. Two people watching out for trouble are better than one.

Maintaining my innocence,

Pilate

Man to Woman

When men have women in their lives who can see what they often don't, they are blessed. And vice versa. Women have a special sensitivity, a special sense of discernment that is unexplainable but usually on target. They have a sense of knowing that can't be easily waved away. If men aren't careful, they can pooh-pooh their women's inclinations away. Time has proven that what women feel about any given situation is usually accurate. Men feel more secure when they know their women have their backs. They covet their women's prayers and input when faced with difficult decisions.

With men, timing is everything. A woman shouldn't give input just for input's sake. She needs to be timely and concise, and give her insights in a manner he will receive. She needs to have nurtured a trust level with her man. What does this mean? You need to choose your battles. Reserve some of your thoughts and feelings for situations when your input really counts. Make sure you're accurate with your well-thought-out disclosures and be sure that God has given you the knowledge. What you want is a track record of giving good advice. Your man doesn't need your opinion on every little thing, so just give it on the things that matter and affect the bottom line of your life together.

Being interested in your man—what's going on with him—and

displaying genuine concern for his work and the things that impact him are ways to build trust and a sense of partnership. With that established, when you feel led to share with him, he'll be more inclined to listen and take your counsel to heart.

It doesn't matter how good your advice is if he refuses to act on what you've said. And his willingness depends a lot on you.

The Truth of the Matter

A few women have made it difficult for the rest of us. You know the ones—those who feel the need to correct, browbeat, and emasculate men. They cause men to be generally distrustful and fearful of us. Color that with a healthy dose of disrespect on both sides, and there is very little material to build healthy bridges between men and women. But as I've pointed out, we were created to be "help meets" to the men God assigned us.[3] God knew that man could not complete the tasks assigned to him in life without help. He created woman to be the completion the man needed. Never underestimate your power in the life of any man, be it a relative, mate, or friend.

The adage "Behind every great man is a woman" isn't spouted for nothing. It's true. It's the precedent a mother set in motion during the early life of her son. He expects support from the woman—and women—in his world. That means having his back. Partnering with him in his life endeavors. Being a force that empowers him to do what he was created to do. The heart of a man rests in the knowledge that his woman backs him up.

The more invested she is in his work and the challenges he faces, the more he gains confidence that he can do what he needs to have victory in his life. Her support becomes his fuel and the impetus for him to be fruitful in his endeavors. Her trust in him solidifies his commitment not to disappoint her. He will move heaven and earth to prove her belief in him wasn't wasted. He will work tirelessly to earn her trust if he knows the reward at the end of the day is her love, honor, and support.

He isn't opposed to direction, correction, or a word fitly spoken into his life. He's open to suggestions. Just be aware of how words are spoken and the spirit behind what's being suggested. Queen Esther was a master at this. She couched her needs carefully when requesting that the king extinguish the enemies of Israel. She presented the matter in light of what it would cost him. She removed herself from the equation and made it all about him. I don't think she did this from a heart of manipulation. I believe her intentions were pure. What it shows me is that we need to examine our motivations for the things we tell the men in our lives. Is it about us or is it about making them the best that they can be? Everyone can smell selfish ambition. Let's make sure we are coming from a pure place of simply wanting to empower our men to be in the right place with God so all else will fall into place. In the end, when our men rise to the occasion and heed sound counsel it works to the good for everyone involved.

Matters of the Heart

1. In what ways can you cultivate a trusting atmosphere between the man in your life and you that will help him be open to receiving your counsel?

2. In what ways have you contributed to a breach in a past communication? How did you correct the situation?

3. How does the man in your life view your counsel? How can you be more instrumental in helping him move forward in God's will?

Women Who Pray

My dear,

I want you to know where your true power lies. In my travels spreading the good news of Jesus Christ, I've been blessed to cross the paths of many women who were zealous in their pursuit of God. But the one who stands out in my mind was Lydia. My companions and I met her when we went down to Philippi. On the Sabbath, we headed down to the river to find a place to pray. We were blessed to find a group of women who had gathered to pray there. Among them was a very successful woman, a trader of purple cloth. Her name was Lydia. She was devout and so open to the things of God.[1] She embraced all we shared and submitted herself and her household to be baptized. She then insisted that we be her guests. At first we declined, but she persisted, saying if we believed she was a follower of the Lord we would accept her invitation. How could we say no to that?

She was a woman of great faith who had mastered the balance of working in the secular world but not allowing it to affect her walk with God. Though she was established in her thriving business and well-known as a successful entrepreneur and woman of wealth, she remained humble and focused on her relationship with God. She was a woman given to prayer and going daily to meet with other believers. Her reputation as a believer in God and a woman of integrity was solid. She was generous and open with all she had. What a heart of service, and she was a very gracious host.

Silas and I had settled in and were busy effecting the work of the ministry by going with her to prayer every day. On the way, a slave girl who had the ability to tell the future followed us often, shouting at the top of her lungs, "These men are servants of the Most High God, who proclaim to us the way of salvation."[2] She was always causing chaos, and her presence was disturbing. I could tell her outbursts were demonic in nature. She wasn't about the business of glorifying God; rather, she was being a distraction. Finally I turned to her and, in the name of Jesus Christ, commanded the demon that operated through her to leave. Immediately she was delivered! However her power of fortune-telling was finished.

Her owners were angry as they considered the loss of revenue due to her deliverance. They caused a major disturbance and incited the crowd to bring accusations against Silas and me. As we were being arrested, I saw Lydia's face. She was as calm as ever. Her lips were moving, and I knew she was praying. Silas and I were hauled before the city officials, beaten, and then thrown into jail. I was sure that this very night Lydia's house would be filled with people praying for our safety and release. I knew God would hear them and us.

So there we were, Silas and I, in prison and singing hymns and praying, waiting in the presence of the Lord to see what He would do. The other prisoners were listening. I possessed a strange peace about the entire situation. I imagined Lydia and the others praying along with us. I knew their prayers were effectual because I'd witnessed their prayer meetings. But most of all, I knew the power of

God to move in amazing ways. So Silas and I were singing songs of praise and thanksgiving when, around midnight, an earthquake shook the place where we were to its very foundation. I felt no fear as the prison doors flew open and the chains fell off. The jailer woke up and saw the doors opened. He assumed we'd escaped and drew his sword to kill himself. I cried out to stop him, telling him we were all still here.

He ran into our cell and brought us out. He fell to his knees as he asked what he must do to be saved. He took us to his home, and we shared the gospel of Jesus Christ with him and his household. He and his entire family wanted to be baptized! This same jailer took care of us by washing our wounds and feeding us. And this was just the beginning of the miracles that occurred.

Bright and early the next morning, the city officials sent the police to tell us we were released and should go on our way...just like that. But we stayed. I reminded the guards that we were Roman citizens who had been wrongly mistreated, and how could they expect us to just slink away? They panicked when they realized we were Roman citizens. The city officials came running to apologize. They assured us they were extremely sorry. They didn't want any trouble. We were free to leave. They encouraged us to leave the city so they could avoid any more upheavals and chaos.

That was fine by me, but we had to make one stop first. We made our way back to Lydia's house to show ourselves to them and give thanks for their vigilant prayers. We were proof that God hears the prayers of His servants. We recounted the events of the evening. The miraculous earthquake that freed the prisoners. The more miraculous conversion of the jailer and all in his household. The surprising turn of events when the city officials apologized and asked us nicely to leave. Everything that happened had God's hands all over it. It was so incredible to believe, and yet there we were. Again they prayed for us, and we prayed for them. That God would keep them. That their prayers would continue to have major impacts in their city. That the power of God would be felt by many.

There is a powerful witness in seeing a woman who is successful in her own right and so trusting and dependent on God. There is a delicate balance between works and faith, and Lydia managed to balance them both in a compelling way. If only all women would master that. In today's "make it happen" world, it's easy to get caught up in qualifications and natural connections to solve critical issues. It's important, however, to know that it is *God* who prevails for us. Prayer is essential, and people who know how to pray can be a mighty force.

Prayerfully,

Paul the Apostle

Man to Woman

Every man longs for a woman who will move heaven in prayer on his behalf, whether she be wife, sister, mother, or friend. Men know that things happen when women pray. They sometimes believe God has a special affinity for women. Or perhaps they attribute it to the position women often take that allows God to be God in their lives. A woman who is successful yet still totally dependent on God is beautiful. There is something very disarming about a woman who is both powerful and vulnerable at the same time. She's aware that the source of her power and influence lies in God—and in Him alone. Every man needs a praying woman in his life. His life may add up to the accumulation of prayers that his grandmother, mother, sister, aunt, and wife uttered over him that kept him from seen and unseen dangers.

A godly man doesn't resent his woman being successful. Neither is he intimidated by her victories in the marketplace. He easily rejoices at her victories when she accepts them in balance by giving all the glory to God and keeping her achievements in perspective. This increases her appeal. He feels free to depend on her being there for him and vice versa. Keeping God as the center of every success removes competition from the equation and puts the man and woman on an even playing field. They can share every victory equally because neither takes credit for what has been accomplished. They both know everything they point to has been birthed by prayer and empowered by God.

A woman who prays has the trust of her man. He knows that if she is answerable to God, she will walk in a way that will bring blessings to his life. This helps him face the world with confidence, knowing that he isn't walking alone. He is aligned with heaven. And though he also prays for himself, he depends on the prayers of the woman in his life to cover the areas that aren't apparent to him. He knows God may provide insights to him through his woman. And her heightened sensitivity to his needs allows her to take his concerns to the Father through prayer.

Though a woman may be savvy in business and brilliant in the marketplace, the man in her life knows the most powerful weapon she wields is her capacity to pray for him, even storming heaven on his behalf if need be.

The Truth of the Matter

There is something special about a woman who is known for prayer. Many years ago there was a book written called *What Happens When Women Pray* by Evelyn Christenson. It spoke of the power that women have by approaching God. A praying woman sees miracles. She is the master of the effectual and fervent prayer that avails much. A woman who is willing to go to God to pray for the man in her life and intercede on behalf of others is more powerful than any maven in the secular world.

We can see the power of prayer in full force in Paul's life and in Peter's. When Paul was in jail and others lifted up prayers, he was released from jail supernaturally. When Peter was bound in jail, it was the prayers of the church that helped him get out of jail supernaturally via the intervention of an angel.[3] I believe the metaphor isn't accidental in these stories. Jail represents a holding place where a person can't experience freedom. They are bound and can't free themselves. In many cases in life, this is true for people we know— loved ones, coworkers, friends. When they can't free themselves, the power of release is in your prayers on their behalf. Some of the most powerful words Jesus ever spoke to His disciple Peter were, "Satan has asked for you, that he may sift you as wheat. But I have prayed for you, that your faith should not fail; and when you have returned to Me, strengthen your brethren."[4]

Never underestimate the power of prayer! Sometimes the outcome can be so amazing that even though we prayed, we can't believe the outcome. "To Him who is able to do exceedingly abundantly above all that we ask or think...to Him be glory."[5] After all of our amazing accomplishments and wonderful acquisitions that may impress those around us, the thing that impresses God the most and makes our loved ones rest easier is the knowledge that we know how to get prayers through to the heavenly throne room. Part of your assignment from God is to cover the man in your life in prayer. Never stop praying!

Matters of the Heart

1. When a crisis hits, what is your first reaction? How much do you focus on loved ones during your prayer time?

2. How do you balance your "natural" success with your spiritual walk?

3. Why is prayer essential in your dealings, whether professional or personal? What do you need to do to strengthen your prayer life?

The Coveted Bride

My beloved,

The things I want to impart to you would take an eternity to tell. From the beginning of time, I've longed to be in fellowship with you. Before you were, I was. Even now I'm longing to be with you. Before the first day in time as you know it, I had you in My heart. As My Father formed you from the rib of the man, I was enamored with you. I loved you. I watched over you as you slept. I looked forward to every morning when you arose. I anticipated every conversation we would have and desired to be close to you in ways beyond your imaginings. I lived for you. I died for you. I'm waiting for you.

Our history is a long and complicated one filled with intrigue and adventure, passion and deep disappointment, and I intend to redeem every second. As a matter of fact, I have already done so.

From the moment you became unfaithful, I set my sights on winning you back. I was grieved to watch the enemy of your soul bruise you time and time again with distractions that shattered your faith and took you away from Me. Satan, the great deceiver, has lied to you about what is really important. His goal is to sever our relationship, and he does a good job of bringing confusion and separation between us...for a time. But I will prevail. Every day I purpose to prove My love to you and win you back so we might be one. That is My deepest desire, My love—that we be one. That we be inseparable. And when your special man comes along and you join with him through marriage, we'll be a three-strand cord not easily broken. We'll live in union with My Father even as the Holy Spirit, the Father, and I are one. We can't be separated, and that is My desire for you and Me.

I understand you live in the world, but remember you are not of the world.[1] You belong to Me. I am your husband.[2] You are My bride. I am waiting with great eagerness for our wedding feast so I can present you to My Father.[3] What a glorious day that will be! All of heaven will witness our coming together as one forever and ever.[4]

Until then, I will continue to pursue you as an ardent lover pursues the woman he adores. Even when you turn away from Me in pursuit of other lovers, I will remain faithful. I will surround you. My goodness and My mercy will follow after you.[5] My blessings will overtake you. I will draw you out from the things that bind you. I will speak gently to you. I will woo you back. I refuse to let you go.

This is why I left heaven. It wasn't beneath Me to humble Myself, to become temporarily contained in a mortal body to win you back. I know who you can be in all your splendor. Spotless. Without a wrinkle. Clothed in righteousness. Wearing a crown of glory.[6] Glowing in holiness. I see you now as you will be on the day you arrive at heaven's gate.

This is why I fought for you. I battled to the death to redeem you from the hand of the one who has no good intention toward you. I left heaven because I found you worth pursuing. I allowed Myself to be wounded for your transgressions. I was bruised for your iniquity.[7] I took pain and sorrow on your behalf to spare you from these agonizing things. I went to the cross so that we would not be eternally separated. I paid the ransom for your sins so you could never be kidnapped and held helpless in the grip of temptation and evil. I descended to the very pit of hell to redeem you from sin and spiritual death. I snatched the keys of hell and death so you could never be a prisoner of either one.

I ascended to the Father, but I promised I would not leave you comfortless. As the world and the issues of life buffet you, I'm with you through the Helper, the Holy Spirit.[8] When things seem too hard to bear and you find yourself bowed over with your cares—so much so that you don't know how to pray—the Holy Spirit will pray for you, interceding on your behalf in accordance with the will of the Father.[9] And know that I also pray for you continually as I sit at the right-hand of My Father. I feel everything you feel. You are so precious to Me that I even collect your tears.[10] Not one falls to the ground unnoticed by Me. I hold them all. Nothing in your life escapes Me. Sometimes I'm grieved by what I see. Sometimes I stand up and pace so anxious am I for the day when I can take you out of the world.

In the hard times, remember that you are in the world but you will not be contained by it.[11] In a little while, after the will of the Father has been accomplished, I will come and not tarry. Until then, stand fast in the knowledge of My love for you. My love is stronger than death, and I will allow nothing to separate you from Me. No height, no depth, neither death nor life, neither angels nor demons, neither your fears for today or your worries about tomorrow, not even the powers of hell can separate you from My love.[12] No power in the sky above or in the earth below—indeed, nothing in all creation—will ever be able to separate you from the Father's love revealed through Me. I am His expression of His love for you. My Father is love, and in His love for you He gave you Me. I love you with an everlasting love.[13] No one can successfully accuse you before Me. I will cover you because I have paid the penalty for every sin you have done and will do (with the exception of blaspheming the Holy Spirit).[14] Because you have accepted My love for you and called Me Lord, I will forever redeem you from your sins and present you blameless to My Father and Myself.[15]

Do not despair, My love. Life happens. It's the way of the world and the function of living in a place that is unredeemed. So don't feel I no longer love you if you have trouble or calamity, are persecuted or hungry, are destitute or in danger. Despite all these things, overwhelming victory is yours through your relationship with Me because I love you.

I pray for you continually that you will be with Me where I am.[16] In the meantime, I understand that you desire love in a more present and physical form. You were created for love, and I wouldn't expect you to desire less. But far too many times you settle for less than you were created to receive. Remember, I am the husband who waits for you; therefore, I set the standard for what you should accept on earth. Contemplate all that I do and all that I have done for you when considering the man before you. Although he can't be perfect because he is human, he can pursue the standards I've set as your ultimate Bridegroom.

Make sure that he pursues you with My love. Don't give yourself away. I paid a great price for you. Allow him to see your worth. I invested My life for you, so expect your man to want to do the same. Allow him to fight for you. The hunter in him needs to know you are a prize worth fighting for and that should never be taken for granted. He needs to be faithful because I am faithful. Nothing should distract him from you. He should always love you and seek ways to keep love in full bloom.

Though passions may rise, do not stir up love until its time.[17] Remain holy; stay pure. Give him your love at the right time—after both of you have covenanted through marriage to love for better, for worse, for richer, for poorer, in sickness and in health, 'til death do you part. As I lived and died for you, he should be willing to do the same. Settle for no love that is less than what you experience with Me. You want to experience "love, joy, peace, longsuffering, kindness, goodness, faithfulness, gentleness, and self-control."[18] These are the fruits of love. If you don't see these things at work in his life, let go of him. Guard your heart at all times because the condition of your heart affects every aspect of your life.

Read My Word to know what real love looks and feels like. For instance:

> Love is patient and kind. Love is not jealous or boastful or proud or rude. It does not demand its own way. It is not irritable, and it keeps no record of being wronged. It does not rejoice about injustice but rejoices whenever the truth wins out. Love never gives up, never loses faith, is always hopeful, and endures through every circumstance.[19]

This is the standard set by My love for you. This is what I want for you. Someone who will love you as I love you and give of himself as I have done. Be prayerful, careful, and wise when considering love. Don't settle for less. Always remember that you are not alone. I will never leave you nor forsake you. I am with you always.[20] Rest in this until we meet face-to-face.

Forever faithful,

Jesus

Man to Woman

When a man loves a woman, he willingly gives his all for her. He will go to the ends of the earth and back to win her. If your man isn't willing to pursue you, he's not the one for you. This commitment and willingness are two things that separate the men from the boys. A woman needs to recognize the difference.

God places definite traits in male DNA. The man who is for you will know he wants you. He will pursue you. He will have a passion for protecting and providing for you. And when you're in relationship, he will be faithful. If he loves you, he'll be sold out to you. He won't be pulled off course. He'll be determined to let nothing keep you from him. Boaz spotted Ruth and desired to provide for her and protect her even before he really knew her. That speaks volumes about the natural inclinations of a mature man. [21]

When a man is submitted to God, he will know in his heart that you are the one for him. He will call you bone of his bone, flesh of his flesh. His mind is then made up to do whatever he has to do to acquire your hand and make you his own. His love will drive him to do exploits on your behalf and be willing to pay the price for the privilege of being with you. He wants to be your knight in shining armor. He'll slay the dragon for you and shield you with himself. He longs to be your hero, and he'll settle for nothing less if you hold him to it.

A real man is looking for a real woman who knows her worth and walks in the knowledge of it. You are the woman he considers a pearl of great price.

The Truth of the Matter

Jesus loves you, and there is nothing you can do to stop Him. Plain and simple. That's a truth every woman needs to know and embrace. If the Lord of lords loved you unconditionally and invested His very life for your sake, don't lower the bar when it comes to loving the man in your life. Jesus set the standard for love, and you ought to be treated like He treats you. He has given you Himself as an example, and there is no excuse for settling for less than the standard set by Him.

The world has become a desperate place when it comes to the pursuit of love. Though it may be a sign of the last days for seven women to cling to one man, the woman who knows the Lover of her soul doesn't need to be desperate or accept less than the best, which is modeled by God's love for you. Knowing your worth and the value of your love and your body will help you set the best boundaries for your heart and health, as well as keep you on track in your love relationships. God wants you to experience peace, joy, and fulfillment, but you have an active part to play. Based on what you embrace and allow, the outcome will be good or bad.

The first and ultimate love relationship you should invest yourself in is your relationship with God. When you're full and fulfilled in Him, you won't be seeking love in all the wrong places because you'll already be walking in love.

For most men, nothing is more desirable than a woman who isn't looking for love...but is open to considering it. Take the time to rest in your relationship with Christ and get to know Him intimately. He models love for you. Let Him teach you how to love much and love well. This opens the door for you to experience love the way He intended it to be. And that will be as close to heaven as you can get on this earth.

Matters of the Heart

1. What are your expectations of love? In what ways have they been fulfilled? In what ways have you been disappointed?

2. Where has your focus been when it comes to love? Where do your priorities need to be?

3. How is your love life with God? What can you do to improve it? When are you going to start? How will this affect your other relationships?

Notes

What Do Men Really Want?

1. Proverbs 4:5-7.

Chapter 1—The Greatest Gift

1. Ezekiel 28:12-15, 17.

2. Ezekiel 28:13.

3. Luke 10:18.

4. Psalm 8:4.

5. Genesis 2:7.

6. Roswell D. Hitchcock, Rev., "Hitchcock's Bible Names Dictionary" in *Hitchcock's New and Complete Analysis of the Holy Bible*, in PC Study Bible formatted electronic database, © 2003, 2006 by Biblesoft Inc. All rights reserved.

7. Genesis 2:6; 1:29-34.

8. Psalm 8:4-8.

9. Genesis 2:21-22.

10. Genesis 2:17; 3:6.

11. Genesis 3:7.

12. Genesis 3:14.

Chapter 2—The Power of Influence

1. Genesis 2:7.

2. Genesis 2:19-20.

3. Genesis 2:23.

4. Genesis 1:28.

5. Genesis 3:6.

6. 1 Timothy 2:14.

Chapter 3—The Beauty of Submission

1. Genesis 12:2.

2. Genesis 12:11-20; Genesis 20.

3. Genesis 17:4.

4. Genesis 17:15.

5. Genesis 17:16.

6. Genesis 17:9-14.

7. Genesis 18:1-2.

8. Genesis 17:17; 18:11-12.

9. Genesis 21:2.

10. Genesis 21:11-14.

Chapter 4—The Heart of a Servant

1. Genesis 24:2-4.

2. Genesis 16:10.

3. Genesis 16:11.

4. Genesis 21:10.

5. Genesis 21:13.

6. Genesis 24:12-14.

7. Genesis 24:26-27.

8. Genesis 15:2.

9. John 13:8-9.

Chapter 5—The Way of a Woman

1. Genesis 24:63.

2. Genesis 25:23-28.

3. James 3:16.

Chapter 6—What Beauty Can't Do

1. Genesis 29:8-10.

2. Genesis 30:1.

3. Genesis 35:16-18.

Chapter 7—How to Win Respect

1. Genesis 37:6.

2. Genesis 37:9.

3. Genesis 39:1.

4. Some of these insights were drawn from the Jewish historian Josephus. Louis H. Feldman, *Josephus's Interpretation of the Bible* (University of California Press/Regents of the University of California, 1998), p. 352.

Chapter 8—A Woman's Strength

1. Judges 4:4.

2. Judges 4:9.

3. Judges 4:14 MSG.

4. Judges 5:4.

5. Judges 5.

Chapter 9—The Price of Control

1. 1 Kings 16:31.

2. 1 Kings 18.

3. 1 Kings 18:38.

4. 1 Kings 21.

5. This insight was partially inspired by an African proverb.

6. 2 Kings 11:1.

7. 2 Kings 9:22.

Chapter 10—The Importance of Wisdom

1. 1 Samuel 18:20-27.

2. 1 Samuel 25.

3. 2 Samuel 6.

Chapter 11—Building a Legacy

1. 2 Samuel 13.

2. 1 Kings 1:1-2.

3. 1 Kings 1:32-34.

4. 1 Kings 2:19.

Chapter 12—The Passion of Purity

1. Song of Songs 6:13.

2. Song of Songs 1:6.

3. Songs of Songs 8:1.

Chapter 13—The Greatest Beauty Secret

1. Esther 2:8.

2. Esther 1:15-19.

3. Esther 4:16.

4. Esther 4:16.

Chapter 14—The Attraction of Redemption

1. Ruth 2:15-16.

2. Ruth 3:11-13.

3. James 4:6.

Chapter 15—A Man's Weakness

1. Judges 14.

2. Judges 15:4-5.

3. Judges 16:17-21.

Chapter 16—The Need for Agreement

1. Proverbs 22:6.

2. Job 1.

3. Job 1:21.

4. Job 38.

5. Proverbs 14:1.

6. Proverbs 21:9.

7. Ephesians 5:33.

8. 2 Samuel 6:20-23.

Chapter 17—The Price of Love

1. Hosea 1:2.
2. Hosea 2:2-3.
3. Hosea 2:8.
4. Hosea 4.
5. Hosea 6:6.
6. Hosea 3.

Chapter 18—What Faith Can Birth

1. Luke 1:26-38.
2. Matthew 1:20-24.
3. Matthew 2:13-15.
4. Genesis 2:18 KJV.

Chapter 19—The Price of Guilt

1. Mathew 14:2-5.
2. The book of Esther.

Chapter 20—The Power of Spoken Words

1. Luke 1:13-17.
2. Luke 1:19-20.
3. Matthew 12:34.

Chapter 21—How to Change a Man

1. John 4:39.
2. John 4:42.
3. 1 Peter 3:1-2.

Chapter 22—A Woman Who Dreams

1. Luke 23:1-7, 11.
2. Isaiah 53:2-3 NIV.
3. Genesis 2:18 KJV.

Chapter 23—Women Who Pray

1. Acts 16:12-14.
2. Acts 16:17.

3. Acts 12:5-11.
4. Acts 12:31-32.
5. Ephesians 3:20.

Chapter 24—The Coveted Bride

1. 1 John 2:15-16.
2. Isaiah 54:5.
3. Isaiah 62:5.
4. Revelation 19:7, 9.
5. Psalm 23:6.
6. Psalm 132:9; 1 Peter 5:4.
7. Isaiah 53.
8. John 16:7-15.
9. Romans 8:26-27.
10. Psalm 56:8.
11. John 17:13-16.
12. Romans 8:38-39.
13. Jeremiah 31:3.
14. Jesus said, "Whoever blasphemes against the Holy Spirit never has forgiveness, but is guilty of an eternal sin" (Mark 3:29).
15. Colossians 1:22.
16. John 14:1-4.
17. Song of Songs 2:7.
18. Galatians 5:22-23.
19. 1 Corinthians 13:4-7 NLT.
20. Matthew 28:20.
21. Book of Ruth.

More Encouraging Books by Michelle McKinney Hammond

To learn more about books by Michelle McKinney Hammond
and to read sample chapters, log on to:
www.HarvestHousePublishers.com

HARVEST HOUSE PUBLISHERS
EUGENE, OREGON

michelle mckinney hammond

The Power of Being a Woman

Secrets to Getting the Life You Want and the Love You Need

What Are You Looking For?

Romance? Healthy relationships? Success? Bestselling author and businesswoman Michelle McKinney Hammond can help. After exploring the positive attributes God gives to you as a woman, Michelle goes on to help you discover your own unique gifts and talents. With this firm foundation, she reveals how you can move forward confidently, using your new understanding and skills to

- ✼ influence rather than challenge
- ✼ master the balance between your personal and professional life
- ✼ experience harmony and passion in love
- ✼ effectively achieve your goals
- ✼ move mountains with your faith

Enthusiastic, outspoken, and entertaining, Michelle lives what she teaches. Let her help you experience the vibrant life God planned for you!

> *"[Michelle] calls a truce between the genders with her biblically based perspective on the art of being a woman."*
> Today's Christian Woman

Proverbs 31 Wisdom for Living, Loving, and Overcoming

Bestselling author Michelle McKinney Hammond invites you on a lively journey through the wisdom of Proverbs 31. Amid upbeat and inspiring stories, you'll discover intriguing questions that will help you learn more about who you are and where you're going. You'll also discover how you can...

- explore and enjoy every aspect of the season of life you're in
- live up to your full potential and be who God created you to be
- have a greater, more positive impact on people around you
- handle disappointments and get back on track
- develop and nurture rich relationships

With enthusiasm and plenty of encouragement, Michelle offers biblical truths and valuable insights you can use to grow spiritually and make your life more dynamic and fulfilling.

For more information on

Michelle McKinney Hammond

Log on to **www.MichelleHammond.com**

For booking information click on the booking tab at
www.MichelleHammond.com

Twitter: @mckinneyhammond
Facebook: Michelle-McKinney-Hammond
YouTube: heartwingmin